Turn It Up!

This is an IndieMosh book

brought to you by MoshPit Publishing
an imprint of Mosher's Business Support Pty Ltd

PO Box 4363
Penrith NSW 2750

indiemosh.com.au

 A catalogue record for this work is available from the National Library of Australia

https://www.nla.gov.au/collections

Title: Turn It Up!

Author: Witheford, Michael

ISBNs: 9781922912237 (paperback)
              9781922912244 (ebook – epub)
              9781922912251 (ebook – Kindle)

Subjects: **BIOGRAPHY & AUTOBIOGRAPHY**/ music
              MUSIC/ Genres & Styles / Rock; History & Criticism

This book is memoir. It reflects the author's present recollections of experiences over time. All persons within are actual individuals; there are no composite characters.

Cover concept by Michael Witheford

Cover design and layout by Sarah Davies at www.instagram.com/lemon.design.studios

Cover images used under licence from FreePik.

Turn It Up!

Michael Witheford

Also by Michael Witheford:

Buzzed

The Very Worst of The Beatles

Praise for *Buzzed*:

The momentum starts on page one, and never lets up.

The Age

Buzzed should sell for its charm, wit and integrity.

The Mercury, Hobart

A genuine rib-tickler, will leave you smiling. Buy it.

New Woman

Gives Nick Hornby and Tony Parsons a run for their money

Marie Claire

It's hilarious. There are moments of great levity and great truths too.

Who Magazine

A cut above the usual Gen X Tales. Immediate and compelling. Michael has swapped his guitar for a blank page with aplomb. An enviable achievement.

Sunday Sun

For Martin Witheford
(1960-2020)

Introduction

When I was thirteen my mother dropped my brother Martin and I off at the front gates of the local football stadium so we could attend our first gig. Getting a lift to a concert from your Mum doesn't exactly scream rock credibility, but then *you* quite possibly attended your first concert with your parents sitting next to you, which is clearly far less cool.

I had just entered that world where music seems to mean everything (and therefore exploring in the bush or catching tadpoles becomes idiotically pointless) when Ike and Tina Turner somewhat mystifyingly included Launceston on their Australian tour. This was mere months before Tina Turner, battered and abused, escaped from Ike Turner's controlling paranoia and never looked back. On this day though the Turners were together onstage as they had been for many years. The 'stage', in a local agricultural touch, was the large cowpat-stained flat tray of a semi-trailer. There was no backdrop, and since the concert started in the afternoon, no lights or other pyro shenanigans. It hardly mattered. Tina was like a human blast furnace.

'Are you ready for me?' she asked lasciviously. 'Because I'm ready for you.'

Being too young to really understand what a 'groove' was, I imagine I didn't properly appreciate what was going on during the older deep cuts, but they played 'Acid Queen', from The Who's 'rock opera' *Tommy* (Turner was in the movie) and that was the tune I was hanging out for, rather than 'River Deep, Mountain High' or 'Proud Mary' or even 'Nutbush.'

In keeping with his reputation, Ike was not happy that he was met at the airport by a large Ford Fairlane rather than a stretch-limo, and he demanded a pre-gig retainer of ten-thousand dollars in cash, probably greenbacks. In any case, there he was, green skivvy, dark shades, unsmiling, looking like a terrifying militant, or a pimp, or a rogue ex-cop avenger tooled up with a Magnum. Those were the only African-Americans I had seen who looked as intimidating as Ike Turner (and all on TV in blaxploitation movies.)

Anyone who got to see the collective fleshy fireball that was the Ikettes in full flight that day was fortunate indeed. Dressed in hot rouge rags which looked like the seductive undergarments of a Bond villainess, they silhouetted Tina's molten dance breaks and left you feeling that the whole venue would never regain its sporting innocence unless somebody came along and performed a post-gig exorcism.

In later years I would have probably dissected the concert instrument by instrument, but being so young it was more like a brief visit to a strange and oddly arousing planet.

In the subsequent years my own love of music transferred from being a listener to a critic to a performer and less than ten years later I too played music at the same footy ground (now UTAS Stadium) albeit not as the star attraction, in a two-day festival.

In a moment of wistful irony, and because she wanted to take advantage of the rare opportunity to watch us play (due to her not being the type to frequent goth clubs in dungeons) Mum came down to watch us, and I dropped *her* (and Dad) off at the gates of the stadium (with their free passes of course.)

As we took to the stage that day and as I looked out across the relaxed sun-lovers on the field watching us play, and the bobbing heads in the shade of the stands, and the glare of the sun reflected from the silvery floodlights, I thought to myself, 'This was the view Tina Turner had.' And also 'Hey! I can see my house from here.'

Music has a way of unlocking memories that might otherwise be unreliable or murky. Music is specific and sharp and always in focus. It's that song you thought you'd never heard before which you can suddenly sing along to. The dependable record you play when the hundreds of other records you own seem weirdly unappealing. It's the sudden return to a time and place; the smells, the sunlight, the hopes and fears. The mind jettisons the memories it has no use for, but tenaciously hangs on to every pop song that made you lean forward, fully absorbed and in a deep transport. There are experiences we wish we could forget, and others we consciously remind ourselves of as encouragement. Little triumphs. But music is just there. We don't have to worry that it will slip away, or be crowded out by problems or complications or the vagaries of the present. Music buzzes around our neurotransmitters. It is the most powerful example of the beautiful and mysterious machinations of emotion and nostalgia.

1

Although the two things may not have been directly linked, as soon as I hit puberty, I wanted to go to gigs all the time. But gigs (for 'all ages') were quarterly events at best in Launceston. After Ike and Tina, I saw Australian glam-rock wannabes Hush, whose showmanship made up to some degree for the fact that they had no songs and had relied on covers like 'Glad All Over' and 'Bony Moronie' to wedge their way into the charts. The gig ended with bassist Rick Lum and guitarist Les Gock shooting fire and sparklers out of their guitars. But y'know, so what? I guess it *was* the '70s.

There were certainly worse bands on the scene than the pedestrian Hush. In their bare chest kimonos and shiny flares they were a perfect fit for colour TV and therefore for a TV pop show like the legendary Countdown. Tunes now needed to be short, sharp and to the point, to keep the attention of tween and teenage girls.

The chief beneficiaries of what would be a changing of the guard were Skyhooks. Everything about them was on the money. Plenty of make-up, feather boas, top hats, satin jump suits. The songs though, even when couched in kinetic pop-riffs and irresistible melodies were extraordinarily subversive. Thus a strange situation developed where the band developed a fanbase of teens while simultaneously having five of the songs on their debut LP *Livin' In The 70s* banned from commercial radio for taking on subject matter such as masturbation, gay clubbing, stalking, and drug dealing. When adult radio station 2JJ flicked the on switch the first track they played was 'You Just Like Me Cos I'm Good In Bed' by Skyhooks. Their popularity was unusually broad. The material was also site-specific, honing in on various inner Melbourne suburbs. Bassist Greg Macainsh was responsible for most of this envelope-pushing stuff. It was truly unique, and Skyhooks took a rocket trip to the top of the charts for almost four months. The follow up LP *Ego Is Not A Dirty Word* was similarly huge, but the group faded fast when original members Red Symons and Shirley Strachan (strangely) left the band for other gigs in the media. Reunions provided the group with a second wind and a 1990 number one (Jukebox In Siberia), but the zeitgeist had run its course, and there was a novelty element to the band's brief reemergence.

The three-minute pop song delivered a death blow to the beardy, dandruffed, indulgent hippies of the early '70s Australian rock scene. Bands like Chain, Buffalo, Mackenzie Theory and Madder Lake with their loyal and older blues-loving fanbases didn't just roll over and die, but now seemed vaguely archaic and irrelevant. As out of sync as the black and white film clips of their interminable songs, which were aired on a short magazine music and 'issues' TV show called GTK every night at 6.30 pm. I could understand my father being … I suppose disgusted is the right word, by the bands on GTK, but they did nothing for me either. If they were the dinosaurs, Countdown was the massive asteroid they never saw coming.

My earliest exposure to music was naturally via the radio and there are a few specific songs which for some reason impacted on me with a vivid power when I was only 6 or 7. Two were by Petula Clark – 'Downtown', and 'Don't Sleep In The Subway'. My vision of a subway wasn't an underground train station, but instead a piece of large concrete piping on a building site. Now, if you consider the shape of said pipe and the shape of a London tube station (the same thing as a New York subway) they're actually pretty similar – it's just that one is bigger. So I was somewhere in the ball park. The song itself, I thought at the time, was a bit mean, especially if the guy was homeless. Where else was he supposed to sleep? I didn't twig that he was in the subway because he'd had an argument with his lover and she was saying, 'come back, silly boy.' In fact, I had to listen to it again just then to actually work that one out.

Either Clark monopolised the radio of my childhood to the exclusion of mostly everyone else, or I had a particular affinity for her grandly-orchestrated pop songs, because there was also 'I Know a Place', 'Colour My World' and 'Love Here Is My Song' amongst others, which all seem to be seared into my emotional memory banks. I suspect her heyday coincided with the years when I became receptive to pop music. I must have been a weird kid, standing completely still if a song I liked came on the radio. Our radio was a Bakelite relic, an object of vintage curiosity, even in the '60s, but indestructible and able to pick up a thousand stations from all over the world – and there was a transistor radio too, for trips to the beach.

Another solo female orchestral pop star I quite liked was Cilla Black, a prolific hitmaker in the '60s, sponsored by The Beatles who wrote her some songs, one of which, 'Step Inside Love' (by McCartney) became her signature tune. I was allowed to get up from bed (probably at 9.30 pm) to watch Cilla's variety show, where her guests ranged from Tom Jones to Marc Bolan. Cilla was my first crush. It wasn't just the music. There was a yearning too that I didn't quite understand.

'Wichita Lineman' by Glenn Campbell (written by the scarily gifted Jimmy Webb) was another amazingly evocative song. Even a kid can be transfixed by the lyric and the vision of a man strapped to the top of a power pole sorting out the wiring. It never occurred to me that this was not the typical subject matter for a pop song, or that there was a subtext there about separation and whether love would survive it, but when my family would drive to Tasmania's East Coast for our summer holidays, I'd lay on the back seat and watch the power lines dip and tauten, dip and tauten as they stretched between the poles, and I'd hum 'Wichita Lineman.'

Jimmy Webb and I apparently had a kind of weird connection because two of the other songs which painted vivid portraits in my young mind were, 'By The Time I Get To Phoenix' and 'Galveston', both of which he wrote for Campbell. I think the introduction of exotic place names would trigger something in me, even though, at the time, the city of Galveston was renowned for smelling of dead fish, dead petrels and petrol. Asked to describe Galveston in one word, you might say 'Flammable.'

The other song which, if I hear it now, takes me back to a time when every moment seemed loaded with a starburst of joy and security (as opposed to fretfulness over power bills) is 'My Sweet Lord' by that guy from The Beatles. Some songs you hear so much that any feeling of a specific time and place with which you associate them is rubbed smooth. But 'My Sweet Lord' still takes me back to the summer of 1971 and a family break at the seaside, the scent of smoked flathead, the sting of sunburn, and a badly tuned black and white TV.

I should add that the '60s and the early '70s were a nightmare for Australian music. Bands covered hits from overseas with as much verisimilitude as possible. Middle of the road crooners, choked by shiny cravats, somehow remained a staple. The first surprising and original song was Russell Morris's 'The Real Thing' at the end of the decade.

The only decent bands hotfooted it to the UK. The Easybeats met in Australia but were essentially Dutch/Scottish, but certainly cut their chops and hit with a vengeance locally before leaving. The Bee Gees lived in Brisbane for a bit, so not that Australian really. The Seekers though were a truly Australian band, and a brilliant one at that. I have to confess that I don't remember the band hogging the radio or impacting on me as much at the time as they did later. In 1965 however, the rest of the world was smitten.

A folk outfit who began playing to pipe-smoking men with goatees and women in woolly jumpers at clubs in Melbourne, the group made what was initially to be a short experimental trip to the UK, paying their way by playing shows on the same ship which brought my family out from England, the *Fairsky*. Signing up with a talent agency, and hooking up with Tom Springfield, the brother of Dusty, they were presented with some killer pop songs, the first of which 'I'll Never Find Another You', championed by offshore floating broadcaster Radio Caroline effortlessly rose to number 1 in the UK and Australia and number 5 in the US. Their reconnaissance trip to London was now extended indefinitely.

The Seekers were an anomaly in the swinging '60s. Buttoned down and tidy they weren't the kind of band to break a sweat or set teenage hearts a'flutter. But in Judith Durham they had a deadly weapon – the purest and most devastating voice in pop history. Aided by three handsome men whose own vocal chops and acoustic guitars were not to be underestimated, The Seekers made the very difficult crossover between pop and folk look very easy. They were voted the best New Act of 1964 in the NME and played a poll-winners show with the Beatles and Stones. It was like the space-time continuum had fractured. Their next single 'A World Of Our Own' was a top 5 hit, and then came the staggering 'The Carnival Is Over', a Russian folk song adapted by Springfield which booted The Beatles 'Ticket To Ride' off the top of the UK charts. As much as the "baby please don't go" trope is the central theme of a gazillion tunes, nothing had ever captured the exquisite pain of having to let someone go like this. It was like Durham (as the proxy lover) was punching a hole in your chest and tearing out your heart. At one point the song was selling 100 thousand copies a week in England.

More hits followed and there was an Academy Award nomination for 'Georgy Girl'. Back home, 200 thousand people packed into the Myer Music Bowl to see the group play for half an hour. Durham left the band in 1967 to explore new avenues, but there were reunions and LPs in the '90s. I interviewed Judith Durham in 2011 and we mostly talked about the *Fairsky* and my Mum, who wasn't well. Judith died in 2022.

I was not of the generation where Mum and Dad played me their records or influenced my taste. Neither was very interested in music. Dad was sceptical or downright hostile to some of the music I embraced in the years to come when I began my quest to hear everything. He was in his thirties when the Beatles broke out and, understandably I suppose, was less than impressed initially. It was best not to play my metal/hard rock stuff in his presence, and naturally, had he heard my New Wave LPs in the late '70s he might have binned them. Dad tended towards crooners who smoked pipes and wore goatees, and often sat in rocking-chairs wearing cardigans, even in their youthful '30s.

It was ironic because Dad and Mum both had a non-specific musical talent. Neither had learnt an instrument, but Dad had a strong and tuneful voice, and enjoyed singing. Mum had a good ear for a tune and both were excellent dancers. I was hardly their Mozart baby, but they passed on to my brother and I a certain affinity with the workings of music, reasonable voices, and later on a degree of showy-offiness on stage which maybe came from Dad's confidence as a speaker, and Mum's time on a teenage chorus line. (She was forbidden from pursuing this activity in London which was a huge disappointment to her.)

In the early '70s, while still at primary school, I auditioned for, and was chosen to be in the local production of *Oliver*. It would be my first singing gig. No sooner had I received the news than my brother decided that he wanted to be in *Oliver* too. It didn't stop there. Dad also decided he'd give it some 'Oom Pah Pah' and began to grow the menacing stubble of an East End grifter for the pub and market scenes. It really annoyed me. Thunder stolen. Even Mum became an usherette. It was an incredibly popular and professional production, and it saddens me that there is no video of it, as there would be these days. The musical director had to try to get a dozen twelve-year-old boys to do as they were told. I think he had a nervous breakdown.

(Ten years later I was asked to take the lead male role in a musical called *The Fantasticks*. The only notable song was the saccharine 'Try To Remember'. It was a shit musical, and I said no thanks. A few years after that the same company put on Cabaret. Now *that* I *was* interested in but was ill and couldn't audition. It's a strange dichotomy – performing musical theatre when you play in a rock band. The idea of going from 'Oklahoma' to 'White Riot' messes with your head. But I was never going to be Hugh Jackman. I'm still a fan though of the classic musicals of the '50s and '60s and would have loved to have been in *West Side Story* if the Launceston Players had ever taken it on.)

Almost everyone of my generation, (and perhaps every generation) grew up on the endless nourishments of The Beatles, even though the band had split, or were about to, when I was introduced to them. Dad did one thing right. He somehow procured a reel-to-reel tape of Beatles hits which I listened to in the dining room, over and over. Along with other tapes of comedians Wayne and Schuster, and satirist Tom Lehrer, whose songs about nuclear war, racism, junkies and Catholicism went over my head a bit but still sounded funny.

I began to buy records when Dad finally took the plunge on a Kriesler '3 in 1' record player in 1974, and my taste was unexceptionally catholic. It was difficult to take an LP for a test run without Spotify or YouTube. The purchases were to some extent a leap of faith based on the following: Was there a song on the album I'd heard or seen on radio and liked? Was the artist reliable and safe? Had the artist been on the cover of a music magazine? Was the LP sleeve a painting by Roger Dean or something similarly alluring? Was it 'classic rock'? Was the artist definitely not Bob Dylan or a band with too many beards, jeans, suits or hats who played 'folky' stuff?

My first record was a Bee Gees album I was given for Christmas. *To Whom It May Concern* had 'Run To Me' on it, and I really liked 'Run To Me'. At some point during the following year, I probably lost interest in the Bee Gees, such was my newly-minted devotion to guitar rock, but my fixation with the Gibbs, which re-emerged a few decades later has become a pretty solid love affair.

The Bee Gees are many things and are loved for many reasons; the voices and harmonies, the tunes, the lush production, Barry's eternal handsomeness. One thing you don't often hear is how someone became a Bee Gees fan because the Bee Gees are profoundly weird. This was something I only discovered when I took a dive into the more obscure material, and also re-visited some of my favourite songs. Even *To Whom etc* … which I thought I'd remember from my youth has a buried track on it called 'Paper Mache, Cabbages And Kings' which I'd clearly lost memory of, and which is a kind of insane pocket symphony. A sort of warped 'Good Vibrations', which periodically changes key, changes tempo and changes mood. It ends with the fading refrain '*Johnny had a bomb and the bomb went bang / Johnny went everywhere.*' WTF? And yet, when you understand that the Bee Gees really didn't give a fuck what people thought of whatever cock-eyed musical schemes they were dreaming up, you'll find something a bit peculiar in many, many Bee Gees songs.

To start with, their first hit was the snappily titled 'New York Mining Disaster 1941'. How on earth did they get *that* past the record company? (Incidentally there was no historically verified disaster.) As soon as the song was picked up by radio it went gangbusters, because it was a cracking tune, but so *melancholy*.

Barry Gibb then wrote one of the greatest of all love songs, 'To Love Somebody', which has been extensively covered, most notably by Janis Joplin, and least convincingly by Keith Urban. Then the band went *off-piste* again and released 'Massachusetts'. Not only a pretty random place to pick for a song – four tricky syllables – but a city none of them had ever been to. This reminds me of Jimmy Webb writing 'Galveston' and also The Partridge Family singing about Albuquerque.

The hits kept coming and included 'I've Got To Get A Message To You' about a guy on death row about to go to the chair, and 'I Started A Joke' which was more three minutes of clinical depression than a conventional pop song. And yet the Bee Gees were pranksters. They've never adequately explained why so many of their songs were so *grim* when the Gibb brothers themselves weren't averse to the excesses of swinging London, and in interviews came across as three blokes doing the cheeky and witty thing as effectively as the Beatles had in 1964.

Eventually, around 1974, the record sales dwindled and there was a ninety-degree turn into funk. It worked a treat. 'Jive Talkin'' and 'Nights On Broadway' introduced a newly tanned Bee Gees with Barry now singing almost exclusively in a sweet falsetto. Between 1975 and 1979 the band had eight US number ones. And they were all genius, except perhaps for 'You Should Be Dancing' which grates a bit.

But I still prefer to listen to the gonzo demos, the flagrantly peculiar material, always hiding new secrets to uncover. When Robin Gibb temporarily left the band, he had a number one in the UK with 'Saved By The Bell', which I would have to guess is the first hit ever to use a drum machine. It's a primitive analog beatbox and sounds like a trout being slapped on a table. The song might have been recorded in a giant water tank. It was a giant hit anyway. Because of the tune. Robin recorded masses of demos which I somehow procured much later. They were mental. The band often chose trippy song titles which had nothing to do with the songs, like 'The Earnest Of Being George' (from *The Importance Of Being Earnest*.) The Bee Gees are the brothers who, even with 2/3 of them sadly gone, keep on giving.

In mid-1975 the family had a holiday in Europe. I wasn't really bothered about the continental Europe stuff. Eiffel tower … meh. Swiss Alps … whatever. England however was a different matter, with its record shops, fashion boutiques, and gorgeous young women. We touched down just as one of the 1970's most popular groups were enjoying their first number one. The Bay City Rollers were not quite bubblegum and not quite rock. They wore tartan ankle freezers and matching shirts. And so did their fans. And in 1975, you couldn't escape the fans. Rollermania was a genuine phenomenon, but was essentially the result of an algorithm designed by their vile manager Tam Paton. The band could play, but their fans couldn't hear them at gigs, and the group couldn't hear themselves either. Which is a shame because I'm quite fond of their records. The sticking point for me in 1975 was that a thirteen-year-old boy admitting he actually like the BCRs would be like admitting you'd killed your granny and buried her in the backyard.

They covered hits from days gone by, as long as they were about teenage girls being in love. 'Bye Bye Baby' which was a Four Seasons song was at number one for eight weeks when the Rollers took it on. The whole schtick was a twee faux-innocence of summer trysts, and old people not understanding.

Bassist Alan Longmuir, who was twenty-seven, was apparently especially uncomfortable with the Rollers appealing to tween girls. So he left. The band had their own TV show, *Shang-a-Lang* where the hysterical studio audience would surge forward onto barriers that I always thought would just have to break scattering injured girls all over the place.

None of the members of the Bay City Rollers ever saw any money, while their manager loafed about in a mansion, and drove a Rolls Royce.

One guy who DID see a lot of money was Elton John. He released the LP *Captain Fantastic and the Brown Dirt Cowboy* not long after we returned to the mother country. I vividly recall listening to it for the first time on an old record player at my auntie's place. I still rate it as the best Elton John LP I still listen to it. The record was autobiographical with lyricist Bernie Taupin looking back to the early days of his collaboration with Elton, and casting a nostalgic (although not rose-coloured) trip down the years. It verged on "concept" album, except filled with tunes which could have all made sturdy singles. I was pretty much sold before I'd even put the record on the turntable, because the sleeve was gorgeous; two booklets (one for lyrics, and one for old photos), and a massive poster. After *Captain Fantastic* I never bought another EJ album. It was strange falling out, but the albums from 76-80 just didn't appeal to me, and after 1980 of course I could barely recall who Elton John was. I think that duet with Kiki Dee didn't help.

1975 though was a time when glam-pop was massive in the UK, and it was all a bit of harmless fun. The Rubettes, Mud, Showaddywaddy, Gary Glitter (and The Glitter Band who were much better without creepy Gary) and Sweet dominated the charts and looked ridiculous in their combination stack-heel silver boots and '50s 'Teddy Boy' coats. Most of the songs were based on a template of doo-wop, with dollops of noisy drums, trashy guitars and hand claps.

Glam is a loaded term, mind you, since there were artists who had embraced the sparkle and fashion but were musically much more sophisticated. Bowie of course, Marc Bolan, Roxy Music. Across the pond Lou Reed was going through an androgynous phase too.

You should have seen me in August 1975 however. I convinced mum and dad that to be a bit of a fashion king I needed absurd high heeled shoes which, if I had kicked someone, would have killed them. I procured voluminous flares, and a tight V-neck jumper with stars all over it. When I returned to Launceston my England outfit was binned, never to be spoken of again. I was back to drainpipe jeans and Golden Breed surf T shirts. Fickle? Moi?

2

Between the ages of twelve and fourteen I began to amass a collection which, for a kid, wasn't too shameful; Elton John, Deep Purple, Alice Cooper, Aerosmith, Wings, The Who, Mott The Hoople, Skyhooks, Thin Lizzy, Led Zeppelin, ELO. With groups like the Sensational Alex Harvey Band I was embracing and at least partially understanding music which, compared to chart pop, was very strange indeed.

Clearly, I favoured the white-men-with-loud-guitars thing, but I made terrible mistakes. Uriah Heep were a godawful English band who combined proto-heavy metal with prog rock and failed dismally at both, but I bought their records because fantasy artist Roger Dean painted their sleeves and because they were white guys with guitars. I bought a few Jethro Tull records – a confusing outfit who looked like hobos in codpieces and featured a flute as their main instrument, except when the white-guys-with-guitars schtick took over.

The Who were a decent enough choice. When I was in England and at the age of twelve, I watched a chat show, on which Pete Townshend talked about heroin addiction. I wasn't sure what heroin was, beyond it having something to do with drugs, and being in most cases fatal. One of the record bars in town ordered in far too many copies of *The Who By Numbers* so I picked it up for two bucks (along with *Sabotage* by Black Sabbath; white guys etc.) It *looked* cheap – a flimsy join-the-dots cover without the pleasing and sturdy gatefold sleeves I tended to equate with good records, but *By Numbers* was in fact an excellent LP. I was more interested in filling in the dots on the 'fill in the dots' cover, and then adorning the sleeve with some colouring-in pencils than listening very hard to great tracks like 'They Are In Love.' The worst song was 'Squeeze Box' the lyrics of which I quickly learnt, blithely ignorant to the double-entendres at play. Hence, one day I sang with gusto, *"Mama's got a squeeze box, daddy never sleeps at night … she goes in and out and in and out"* in the car with my own Mama and Daddy who weren't impressed.

I was too young to understand that most of my favourite bands were, to some extent derivative of artists *they* listened to when they were my age. Almost all had played blues standards or simplistic rock'n'roll before their success and then developed their own identities. I had no idea for example that the Alex Harvey song 'Framed' had been written twenty years before he recorded it by the great Lieber and Stoller and was a veiled reference to police brutality dished out routinely then … and, well now too, on blacks. The song is so similar to 'Riot In Cell Block No 9' mind you, I'm surprised the writers didn't sue themselves. Similarly, unless a Motown song was already familiar to me, I would be none the wiser when it was covered by a rock band. It was mainly a new attention to detail and history as I grew into music that informed me that The Jam's version of 'Heatwave' for example was a cover of a Holland/Dozier/Holland Motown classic as sung (initially) by Martha and The Vandellas (and then by The Supremes and Linda Ronstadt but it was Wikipedia that told me that last one.)

Songwriting teams and individuals have always enjoyed having their songs aired and then covered by as many artists as possible to maximise their financial return. In the case of a tune like 'Yesterday', the original of course was a huge hit for The Beatles (McCartney) but the number of recorded covers stretches to three figures. I've never heard any artist whinge about having one of their songs covered, no matter how execrable the results. Some writers – Carole King, Neil Sedaka – were also performers, and the behemoth of the power ballad, Diane Warren is also a singer of sorts but really shouldn't bother, given her success selling songs and her lack of success singing them herself. With forty-five years of hits under her belt I fail to see how Warren cannot be the richest individual on the planet.

I benefited from having friends who had also dispensed with pre-pubescent amusements like *Mad* magazine and taken to record-buying. Their tastes were dissimilar enough to mine for me to be introduced to a lot of music which I would be unlikely to buy, but which educated me further on my quest to know everything. Dave Bracey, who lived on my street was way ahead of my fairly safe curve, and in his bedroom he played me the Velvet Underground, Lou Reed (he owned the unlistenable *Metal Machine Music*), Roxy Music, The Tubes, Bowie's Berlin trilogy, Iggy Pop and more. Brian Eno's *Taking Tiger Mountain By Strategy* was abrasive and spooky, and would be massively influential on bands like Gang Of Four and Elastica in the days of post-punk. Dave was a kind of art-rock savant-fan. He was fifteen and had the record collection of a twenty-seven-year-old American rock critic.

My friend Graham introduced me to Todd Rundgren and bands from the English Canterbury Scene, the progenitors of which – Caravan and Camel and Hatfield and the North – played whimsical, semi-acoustic, pastoral tunes, best-suited to hippies as accompaniment to them painting their Kombis and heading off to Stonehenge.

Graham was also a devotee of prog-rock, but I could never abide by Genesis or Yes (who my brother also loved … as well as Gary Glitter for some ungodly reason) but I did end up with my own copies of a few Todd and Caravan records.

It makes me wonder just how much pocket money I was being slipped, since I was buying records like a mad person, and also purchasing two or three music magazines a week. It was a fertile time for the papers. NME, Melody Maker and Sounds led the charge in England, and then there was Creem and Circus and Rolling Stone from the US. Top of the pile though was RAM, from Sydney. If the paper didn't arrive in newsagents on the day it was supposed to it felt like a cruel betrayal, a tragedy worthy of Macbeth.

I would read RAM cover to cover, quite literally, and the journos became my heroes as much` as rock stars. I couldn't quite believe my eyes when I had *a letter* published in RAM. Later I would write gig reviews for the college paper, and a decade after that began a career in rock journalism in Melbourne. So I was the wannabe intern, learning the ropes from a distance. Picking up the vibe.

I belonged to a record club, so about half of the music I bought would be delivered to our front door. The sight of an LP-shaped cardboard box behind the flyscreen when I got home from school would induce palpitations. It meant too that the sleeve of the record would be in pristine shape, whereas in 'record bars', the constant thumbing of the browsing public used to bend covers out of shape.

I bought about four or five Monty Python LPs through the record club. Why? How many times can you hear a joke before it loses its piquancy? Twice I would have thought. The most interesting thing about Monty Python records were a) the parodic sleeves and b) the fact that on the *Matching Tie And Handkerchief* album one side had a kind of double groove, so when you dropped the needle it would play either one of two different 'sides'. That was a novelty for about five minutes. It's not that Python weren't hilarious, or even that the records were bad. They were just pointless, and in a way all comedy albums are. Music bears up to repeated listening, but gags don't. I can't say *why* music has this quality, but imagine if it didn't. Imagine if everyone was sick of 'The Long And Winding Road' after listening to it once. Consider what would happen to pop music if everyone who heard a song they liked didn't go out and buy the record because once was enough thank you very much.

Would *Dark Side Of The Moon* still be in the charts after about a hundred years? How big would the crowds be at AC/DC concerts if everyone decided that the band playing their biggest hits would be a BAD THING?

3

There were plenty of bands I kept tabs on as I approached my mid-teens but it was Queen who became my first serious obsession. It may have been 'Bohemian Rhapsody' which was the catapult for most fans, but on reflection that flatulent disjointed and egotistical six minutes of indulgence paled quickly when compared to the first three Queen LPs; *Queen*, *Queen 2*, and *Sheer Heart Attack*.

Queen were cannon fodder for critics who deemed their songs to be a mish-mash of other bands, largely Led Zeppelin, which was fairly wide of the mark. Some of the material in those early records was astonishing. Songs which took off on strange tangents of wild multi-tracked guitar, then eased back like a receding tide for isolated piano parts or acoustic interludes. Freddie Mercury's lyrics were often more focused on fairies at the bottom of your garden and ogres and Black Queens than love, sex, heartbreak or anything typically human. The main thing was that no matter how many songs dealt with the politics of gargoyles coming to life, or however many demented vocal harmonies were introduced, Queen at that time wrote killer melodies.

It's easy enough to see Brian May as a nerdy astronomer who never looked entirely convincing as a guitar hero, but he had a head full of music and a voice which enabled the band to slap rich vocal layers on most of their tunes (relying too on John Deacon, and especially Roger Taylor, whose falsetto first appears at the start of 'Ogre Battle' and is likely to have you screaming in momentary terror if you're not ready for it).

Producer Roy Thomas Baker wisely split the voices and overlapping guitar parts into a full stereo pan. A mono version of *Queen 2* would sound like a head on crash between two garbage trucks.

Sheer Heart Attack is more conventional, albeit with some stunning riffs and great songs like 'Brighton Rock', 'Now I'm Here' and 'Killer Queen' which was the single (and hit) that the record company had been nervously waiting for.

I'd like to keep to the script here and suggest that *A Night At The Opera*, and *A Day At The Races* were bad records, but both had their stellar moments. At this time, as much as Freddie was lapsing into unabashed pastiche verging on parody, he was unable (like McCartney and trifles like 'Your Mother Should Know') to write a bad tune. But the kind of hilarious and often breathtaking madness of *Queen 2* had been shelved.

Documentaries on Mercury tend to lean on Live Aid as a starting point, when for me, that particular trip had ended long before. If the guy was a genius, and he might have been, it wasn't 'Crazy little Thing Called Love' which put him up there.

May and Taylor were also writing horrible songs like 'We Will Rock You', and 'Radio Ga Ga'. This meant nothing to me since I'd jettisoned Queen like useless ballast from my life when they started releasing albums like the execrable *Jazz*. It was the kind of disc that made you want to punch the band in the face. Fortunately, I had New Wave to fall back on, so that was convenient.

Also the other bands I liked had mostly split up, or fallen from favour, releasing LPs nobody really wanted. So I put the brakes on Deep Purple after their pointless second live LP *Made In Europe*. After Thin Lizzy released the excellent *Black Rose*, they failed to be quite as excellent. Phil Lynott, sadly was drinking heavily and into drugs, and the outcome of that was predictable. Still, he could write belters like 'Chinatown' if he wanted to. Also, sad, is that it would cost me the price of admission to discover a band had just sold me a shit LP.

One band I liked, and it's predictable that I would, was ELO. Electric Light Orchestra if you're under 50. ELO were the sort of band that punk had in its crosshairs from the start. They committed many musical sins; they were 'lush', their productions, helmed by front-man Jeff Lynne dripped reverb and echo and tricksy bits and bobs that only he it seemed, knew how to pull off, and they looked pretty bad – beards, satin scarves, flares, long haired-men trying to 'get down' and 'rock out' with cellos. But Lynne was a student of The Beatles, so although there was a lot of flash, in terms of his songs, there was also very little flab. People used to say ELO were the '70s version of The Beatles, and for three LPs they did sound like 'Strawberry Fields Forever' being played by a philharmonic orchestra on mushrooms, but later as their music became less meandering, I heard more Roy Orbison and Beach Boys and Bach in Lynne's songs.

They may have wandered into a minefield by becoming massively popular just as punk was becoming massively popular but they stuck to their guns, and had the temerity in 1977 (of all years) to release a double album, *Out Of The Blue*. It was good, all four sides. It may have helped that the band never entirely shook off their working-class Birmingham roots, because there never seemed to be drug issues, or alcoholism, or general rock shitfuckery, and they never had their own Boeing 707 weighed down by cocaine and groupies. You imagine an ELO groupie to be the kind of girl who'd meet the band and ask if she could play one of their violins. They did emerge onstage from a giant spaceship mind you, but Lynne could always see the Spinal Tap side of things. As well as delighting pop fans, *Out Of The Blue* featured some cross-feed glitterball disco on 'Turn To Stone' with its skittering cellos-from-Good Vibrations intro. ELO went on to pen some tunes for the strange and largely inept Olivia Newton John movie vehicle Xanadu, but the soundtrack was massively popular.

The death knell for me and Queen and ELO I guess, came when I bought *White Music* by XTC. I'd heard their first proper single 'Statue Of Liberty', and then 'This Is Pop', and that was it. Traditional rock suddenly seemed flabby and embarrassing.

My immersion in punk and later New Wave was gradual but eventually comprehensive. *White Music* was an admixture of jagged riffs, mostly unintelligible lyrics – you could sing along to the choruses at least – and some tunes. It was extremely loud. Every instrument seemed to be under assault, punched and kicked rather than being played. XTC's chief songwriter and vocalist Andy Partridge described XTC as "Captain Beefheart meets The Archies" which was about right.

XTC continued to experiment and evolve, and became arguably the first New Wave band to segue into the unexplored territory of pure-pop while maintaining a scathing social conscience. Eventually they more or less entered an area of '60s psychedelia – e.g 'Grass' – and then created a camouflaged band for that very purpose, The Dukes Of Stratosphear. Other bands like The Cure also expanded their minimalist vision of melancholy and despair into more user-friendly and expansive pop. From 'Killing An Arab' to 'Love Cats' in a few years.

Meanwhile groups like the post-Deep-Purple Rainbow, the post-Alex Harvey Sensational Alex Harvey Band (without Alex) (brackets not mine), and the post-Mott The Hoople, British Lions were one at a time replaced by a variety of New Wave bands. I should add that, after he left Mott, Ian Hunter released an amazing debut solo LP with a very poor follow up. Alex Harvey drank himself to an early grave at the age of 47. SAHB were a little disturbing in hindsight. Alex chose very odd songs to cover; 'The Impossible Dream' from *Man Of La Mancha*, Tom Jones's 'Delilah', Jacques Brel's 'Next' and the Hitler youth clarion call from *Cabaret*, 'Tomorrow Belongs To Me' (with the word 'fatherland' removed).

It wasn't necessary to buy the fringe punk LPs. I had a friend called Spike. Spike had 'gone' punk the moment he first witnessed the Pistols on TV. Off went his hair, and on went the chain and padlock. Out went the Kiss records and in came some dreadful punk records by chancers who trailed along in the wake of The Clash and Pistols, The Jam and X Ray Spex. But he did have some cool stuff like Richard Hell so I was always learning, learning, learning.

That short news piece on the upsurge of punk rock in England changed *me* too. Had it not, I'd have stuck determinedly to my guns, and viewed the whole punk palaver in the same way my father did. Which was to turn the TV off before the end.

The one-and-only hit and run album by the Pistols contained all their singles and might otherwise have been considered a bit of a rip off, but it distilled everything the group stood for. Essentially the opening riffs were simplistic (especially after Glen Matlock left) but by Christ they were loud, courtesy of Steve Jones having a number of guitar tracks over-dubbed on every song. All the lead breaks owed a debt to Chuck Berry, but it was still an album you had to own.

Having been sacked by the freaked-out suits at EMI and A&M it was Richard Branson and Virgin who took a chance on the Sex Pistols. And a small label in Australia called Wizard who picked up the local licence. This meant the Sex Pistols were on the same label as Hush. Perfect!

I kept my ears peeled on The Clash, Ultravox (at that time a genuine electronic outfit), the underrated Penetration, and X Ray Spex. In New York CBGBs alumni like The Ramones and Blondie were staples in the music magazines, and that was good enough for me.

It took me decades before I investigated, among others, Neil Young, Joni Mitchell, The Beach Boys, Marvin Gaye (and Motown in general) and Sam Cooke, plus the entire history of country music. Mind you I did get going with Johnny Cash and Hank Williams in my early twenties. But who needed serious music – Hendrix, The Doors, Cream, The Byrds – when New Wave offered so much sheer energy and up to the minute brio? New was the key word. This was happening *now*.

The last band I had to let go of was 10CC. I used to love

10CC, mostly when Lol Crème and Kevin Godley were in the band in the mid-'70s. When the pair left to make their own LPs and later some of the best-known music film clips of the '80s, the remaining version of 10CC became a little 'meh'. The cynical, parodic, pastiche art school angle the band excelled in was ditched, as though the band felt they had to dumb down. Like many groups there was the transitional phase where an album was 'not bad' but would be followed by an LP which was 'very bad indeed'. So when 10CC released *Bloody Tourists* (and the ghastly racist cod-reggae single 'Dreadlock Holiday') I was quietly disappointed. When I bought the 10CC Live LP, I knew I'd just wasted eight dollars … no wait, 15 dollars – it was a double album – on something drab and sad when I could have bought three issues of Playboy instead.

Live albums were essentially without artistic merit, but most bands looking at some filler between proper albums had a crack. For fans, the records were sometimes a way of acquiring new versions of old songs. (New in the sense that they sounded the same, with added crowd noise which was sometimes added later.) Some live albums were exhilarating mind you, and well worth some attention. I probably discovered a few bands in the first instance via live albums; Mott, Alex Harvey, Thin Lizzy's *Live And Dangerous* was a tremendous record too, as was *The Who Live At Leeds*, but some couldn't have been more vapid and exploitative.

When Cheap Trick (who I'll get to in more depth) recorded *At Budokan* they had no idea that the record would be released in any market other than Japan. Even then, for fans who had all the previous LPs, there was enough new music on show to make it a worthwhile release. It was the band's first global hit fuelled by the up-tempo Power Pop version of 'I Want You To Want Me' a very different beast to the honky-tonk, slightly twee original. This was a rare case of actually wanting, or needing, to have both studio and live versions.

Another option for a kind of dip-your-toes in and test the water approach, was the value-packed Best Of or Greatest Hits. The complete acquisition of an artist's discography tended to happen in reverse. You started with the new record and travelled backwards until you got to the debut. Each record was a test case to make sure the 'early stuff' was palatable.

I tried this a bit with Elton John. First the greatest hits, then the hugely underrated *Captain Fantastic And The Brown Dirt Cowboy*, followed by *Goodbye Yellow Brick Road*, and then *Don't Shoot Me I'm Only The Piano Player*. I was wary of earlier efforts like *Tumbleweed Connection* and *Honky Chateau* because the sleeves didn't look glam enough. (Never mind that *Honky Chateau* had 'Rocket Man' on it, as well as 'Honky Cat'.) The LPs prior to that were clearly the work of a piano-playing singer-songwriter, which meant no guitar riffs. Which was a problem. I always thought 'Your Song' was a bit cheesy. I lost interest in Elton's new LPs when I was fourteen. It was a short but intense love affair, and I still play his mid-'70s bangers.

(Being the kind of wide-eared lover of most music when I was 10 or 11, I did however like Paul Williams, Cat Stevens, and James Taylor whose gentle balladry I heard being played at a friend's place by his sister. I tend to equate that time and music with the intensity of the crush I had on her so that might need to be taken into account. You should know that had I the cash I would have bought *everything*, with a minimum of value-comparison or decision-making.)

Within stiff parameters my taste was expanding, if that's not a contradiction. Critical acclaim wasn't really a factor with artists I simply couldn't get interested in; Leonard Cohen, Stevie Wonder, Steely Dan, Santana, Bob Marley. Mega-platinum freakish successes like *Hotel California* were easy to ignore as well. On the grounds of being batshit boring. I resisted the Stones when I was young too. I've thought about the wisdom of this. I think it may have been that the loosey-gooseyrootsy blues-based rock of the world's biggest band lacked the just-add-power-chords pop that most of my records boasted.

I never understood the Elvis thing either. Well, not after he was discharged from the army anyway. I used to babysit for a neighbour who had all his records which I worked through. It was a bit of a slog. Early Elvis footage is extraordinary. It's hard to comprehend the impact he must have had on music and culture in those first 5 years 1955-1960. He more or less invented sex. And he could really sing. But by the early '60s the rock songs – the good ones – had dried up and the guy was starring in movies like *Tickle Me, Clambake and Girl Happy* while releasing singles that were perfectly kid-and-parent friendly. There was one interesting LP, *Elvis Is Back*, which saw him do unusual versions of songs from a variety of sources, but by the end of 1962, Elvis was irrelevant … by choice. But he'd set a match to that rock'n'roll volcano in 1956 and could sit back now and watch it spit fire. When The Beatles and Beach Boys emerged, the sexual threat of the rampant teenage Presley appeared to have not caught on. But there was still Little Richard, Jerry-Lee Lewis, Carl Perkins and Eddie Cochran who was dead at twenty-one in a wrecked car. The Beatles were taking notes, and though they could never be as lascivious (for the public anyway) their effect on crowds of electro-shocked teenage girls was the same. The Stones were the first band whose stage antics and songs might have been described as 'lewd'.

Elvis redeemed his legacy somewhat with the '68 *Comeback* Special', looking hungry and growling through some early rockers. He followed this up with two classic singles, 'In The Ghetto' and 'Suspicious Minds' but by the early '70s he was being poured into a rhinestone jumpsuit and being horse-whipped to play endless shows in Vegas by his terrible manager "Colonel" Tom Parker. But Elvis had become more defiant, and the Vegas concerts featured a variety of material that highlighted Elvis's own broad tastes and not Parker's ideas.

Even near the end, puffy-faced and sweating from a diet of junk food and pills prescribed by a number of doctors, the voice was sometimes the same – indestructible and unwavering. A star burning with its last reserves of fuel and soon to vanish.

4

At the age of fifteen I travelled to Brisbane for a soccer carnival and, on a visit to the city, discovered a record shop which was clearly better than any back in Launceston. Here I bought my first Sparks record. I can't recall if I'd heard Sparks, but the sleeve was sufficiently strange for me to take a punt. The band's name was absent from the front cover which was clearly a reason to pick the album up and find out who they were. Russel Mael was a prototypical rock front man but his brother Ron, with brilliantined hair and forties bank clerk clothes, not to mention what you'd have to describe as 'a Hitler moustache', cut a very strange figure indeed.

The Maels were from California but they'd relocated to England in the early '70s. *Kimono My House* was unlike anything I'd heard – an admixture of hysterical helium-drenched falsetto vocals, prominent keyboard 'riffs', and well, yes, some white guys with guitars. They sang about tactical warfare, sneezing, climate change (presciently) and hating children. I followed the peculiar pop music of Sparks over four more LPs, two more which came before *Kimono*, and two after, then I promptly forgot about them. The group became pioneers of electronica, working with Giorgio Moroder and that was admirable, but by then I was having to stick to the newest of the New Wave.

Sparks never split, never gave up, and never stopped releasing one largely ignored record after another. In recent years they've enjoyed a spectacular renaissance, thanks largely to Edgar Wright's 2021 documentary. Having now released twenty-one (at time of writing) LPs, they are possibly (along with Cheap Trick) the most enduring band ever. I'm not allowing here for groups who take a lengthy hiatus or 'get back together' after years in the wilderness dealing with pecuniary pain.

The influence of Sparks can't be underestimated, which is why I'm banging on about them a bit. When the band embraced electronica, they essentially created a sound which was then pilfered by New Order, Depeche Mode, Erasure and many more. It could be argued that Queen owed something of their eclecticism to early Sparks records. 'Your favourite band's favourite band,' is how they're often described.

I continued to hold prog-rock in a slight disdain. I was the kid who *didn't* buy *Dark Side Of The Moon*. Groups who didn't fit any specific genre, but were in any case quite horrible, like Supertramp were to be avoided at all costs. Considering I liked most things I heard, it's interesting to recall how some music really, really annoyed me. I would have rather listened to someone mowing a lawn full of broken glass or a garbage truck outside my window than an Average White Band album. And they got off lightly.

As a rule of thumb, most rock stars look like they should be rock stars. Elton john didn't, so he changed his image until he did. Mick Jagger would have looked strange wandering around the streets of London and waiting at train stations, but was perfect as a Rolling Stone. I've lost count of the times people have said to me 'Are you in a band', even though I'm not entirely sure what their query is based on. I have some photos of myself with rock stars and it's apparent that they're the ones who seem to have the charismatic glow. When my band supported the Divinyls in 1984, we were backstage when Chrissy Amphlett arrived. It wasn't just that she was recognisable. There was something else. Something larger than life. I felt this sometimes over the years as I met more artists who I'd been sent to interview. None of them looked like they worked at a cement factory or a bank. In a city like Sheffield where most men are a bit overweight, a bit bald, and a bit violent, the only thing you can do if you look like Jarvis Cocker is form a band.

This is why I've recoiled from bands full of chunky, balding men (with frizzy bits at the back) in shocking knitted vests and flared jeans. Guys who look like high school maths teachers. I can't confirm whether everything the Average White Band did was inherently dismal, because I didn't want to risk listening to them. And why would you pick such a defeatist bland name?

I bet my friend Graham has at least one AWB record. He likes music far too much that guy.

5

My own life in music as a member of a 'band' for want of a better word started with the kind of bang I struggled to replicate for the next twenty years.

It was 1978. I was sixteen. Launceston Matric College held a concert for the end of regular classes for the year. It was a kind of bespoke talent quest, attended by … well everyone. I have no recollection of who was involved in the various performances (apart from me) or what they did (apart from me), but it's possible that music students may well have played a Chopin duet on piano and violin, and I now recall my friend Nick doing a Pythonesque sketch with a friend. It was that sort of thing.

Biting off a little more than we could masticate I guess, some friends and I learned (to use a slightly grand expression), and re-wrote the lyrics to that terrible faux-punk travesty which a couple of Sex Pistols recorded with train robber Ronald Biggs. We devoted each verse to a particular teacher, and named ourselves the VD Units after an unfortunate description of some new computer monitors (visual display) by the principal earlier in the year. It was quite a witty idea. The only problem was that our singer forgot all the words. And had a voice like a Tasmanian Devil. Actually, when I say 'only problem' there were several. The drummer had never hit anything (or anyone) in his life. The saving grace for us, having employed a kind of rhythmic antagonist, was that, without microphones on the drums, no-one could hear him. My buddy Andrew (who I met in 1975 and am still close to) saved us. He was a bassist but had no trouble switching to guitar. So, I played bass (as I would later, for many years.)

I can only speculate on the reasons why, at the end of the song, the whole place erupted. Maybe because we were loud –

an incongruity in that environment – or maybe our leather jackets, spiky hair, and decision to spit at the front rows created a pleasingly anarchic ambience. Perhaps the combination of Andrew and I, both of whom actually knew how the song went, made it seem like we were a kick-ass rock band. These days primary school kids are being taught about rock, and high school kids play in garage bands instead of learning complicated scales. But back then, no-one had got past the front door of the stuffy halls with an electric guitar. I often wonder what the students would have made of our performance if we had twenty years of experience under our belt and had been able to really rip the place apart.

In any case, the audience furore was the most addictive sound I'd ever heard. Sadly, for the next few decades, I hunted for that sound again and never quite found it. Yes, I rarely played venues as capacious as the hall at the college (which had a balcony) and yes, the students had probably never heard electric guitars in real life, and yes, there have been subsequent nights in big pubs (800 capacity) where the 'sold out' sign has been posted, and the crowd have been undeniably enthusiastic, but that 'teenage rock star' moment was magical and has never really been replicated. (For the sake of full disclosure, that kind of slightly confusing 800-ticket-sale popularity was mostly confined to Perth and to my time in the Fish John West Reject.)

The crowds may have been a little bigger – pushing a thousand – when we supported The Church and The Violent Femmes. But as second on the bill, you never imagine anyone is there to see you. Similarly, my next band Lust In Space played in front of perhaps 3000 punters in Launceston at the Velodrome in 1995, but that was a day long festival at which we were comparatively minor players. We deliberately moved ourselves down the bill a few places as well in order not to miss the plane back to Melbourne where we were playing that night. This possibly gave us a patina of jet-setting glamour, but was probably just a way of losing money. And in any case, the crowd didn't go nuts like they did in 1978.

Back in the '70s and early '80s, the sheer shock of securing any sort of gig, was far too thrilling for any kind of remuneration to come into it. Anybody who paid to see those nascent, frightful, and spectacularly awful bands of my youth would have demanded a refund whilst pointing a gun at our collective heads.

In any case, it was a year or so after the college triumph before I played once more. 1979 was a year for listening to a plethora of extraordinary records, and attending concerts by the best bands in the country. It was a halcyon period like no other.

In that one winter Launceston was visited by Cold Chisel, Split Enz, The Angels, Skyhooks, Jo Jo Zep, Kevin Borich, Dave Warner's from The Suburbs, Richard Clapton and more. My friends and I would arrive well before the appearance of the support act, let alone the headliners, perhaps to get a table, but also because we had the patience and stamina to spend six hours in a smoky venue listening to 'Knock on Wood' and 'I Was Made For loving You' (the two songs I clearly remember from that time) drinking Mercury cider and making the smoky venue smokier with our Park Drive cigs.

There was something confrontational and almost bullying about the aggression of Cold Chisel. They began with 'Shipping Steel', and it wasn't so much that it was loud through the PA, although it was, as much as the band being loud. Jimmy Barnes sang as though he had no microphone and had to get everyone to hear him anyway, Ian Moss gave his Strat a beating. It felt like a hairdryer being trained on your face. Barnes ended up hanging from the rafters at the back of the venue singing 'Wild Thing'. Don Walker wore a full-face balaclava for the whole show.

The Angels were probably my favourite Australian band at the time, so I stood front and centre while they tore through the exceptional *Face To Face* and *No Exit* albums. Not since the Ramones had a band sounded so much like itself by dishing out an unvarying formula – riff, vocal verse, chorus, key change, lead break, chorus. But what a formula. Before they were adopted (as would also be the case with Chisel) by hordes of rough-hewn suburban and regional young men with utes, The Angels cloaked their twin-guitar attack with a literacy, some keenly observed metaphors and the application of philosophical namechecking which, looking back, gave lie to the adage that 'It's only rock'n'roll'.

When Doc Neeson sang *'Students out to pose in their studied disarray / Books of Sartre, Marcuse openly displayed.'* we were clearly *not* in Ramones territory. Then there was 'Am I Ever Going To See Your Face Again' and the fruity, *'Went down to Santa Fe where Renoir paints on walls.'* Whether this was a graffito allusion, I'm not sure, but in any case, audiences quickly learned to intellectualise things themselves and fill in the chorus gaps with the now famous and expressive, *'No way get fucked fuck off.'*

Towards the end of the show Doc Neeson threw (almost hesitantly) a bucket full of an unknown sticky liquid over me, because I gestured to him that it would be a really great thing to do. I never discovered what it might have been. Possibly three parts water, two parts whisky and one part bodily fluids.

As an aside, the Angels 'borrowed' a Status Quo song called 'Lonely Night' for 'Am I Going To See Your Face Again'. It's a flamboyant and undisguised spot of Grand Theft Music, and yet it does seem that Doc Neeson may have subconsciously heard the Quo song and rewritten it by accident. The Angels eventually settled out of court. And considering the royalties that 'Am I Ever …' still accrues, that wouldn't have been a bad result.

As impressive as Cold Chisel and The Angels were, it was Dave Warner and his band who left the most lasting impression. Warner was an unprepossessing everyman who had released an album called *Mug's Game* which largely bemoaned the luckless life of unbeing unhip in a hip-hip world. This I could relate too. My own perceived lack of good fortune with girls was more due to ineptitude and inexperience than any deep-seated failings, eldritch looks, or off-putting personality traits. But that's not how I saw it.

Warner of course was playing an exaggerated character. He may have experienced some of the brush-offs and nightclub humiliations everyone is bedevilled by, especially when you're young and trying too hard, but he was a rock star now. Rock stars pull, or at the very least, seem to find the right girl without fuss. I was no rock star, and the girls I found devastatingly attractive showed no interest. Hence the expression, 'crush'. Crushed, squished and destroyed.

As the personal spokesperson for my life, Warner lived up to all my hopes. The band played two sets of more than an hour each. I'd have been happy if he never stopped.

The best records of their already impressive canons were released by The Clash, Elvis Costello, Graham Parker, Nick Lowe, Dave Edmunds, The Police, XTC, Blondie (technically *Parallel Lines* was 1978 but easily eclipsed 1979's *Eat To The Beat*), The Buzzcocks, X Ray Spex and The Jam. Each band it seemed had been building up to these releases. I could barely keep up. There was Ian Dury, Lene Lovich and Squeeze as well. The most cherished record for me in that halcyon year was *Shades In Bed* by The Records. Every so often a band comes along who seem to hone in on your personal late teenage zeitgeist and soundtrack it. The songs dealt mostly with unrequited love, which in itself wasn't unusual, but the elements the band borrowed from the early Beatles, The Who, and The Kinks enabled a perfect expression of what's often described (a little carelessly) as Power Pop.

The most exquisitely tuneful and thrilling Records song was 'Starry Eyes', but the lyrics, rather than focusing on some kind of unattainable and heartbreaking girl, were a spiky message to the band's shonky former manager. '*While we were on the beach were you dreaming all about your shares? / Planning to invest in all to cover wear and tear.*' Not much romance there. They should have written a version for their young listeners nursing painful crushes.

The last great record of the decade was *London Calling* by The Clash. I bought it, but I admit, for all its groundbreaking strengths, this double album of many shades and shifts and social commentary didn't appeal to me as The Clash had when they were a punk rock band. This may have seemed naïve but it was easier to play along with the sledgehammer funk-free chords of the *Give 'Em Enough Rope* LP.

As a way of testing this hypothesis, I just listened to both records and feel the same way.

(I've just remembered that around this time John Mayall's Bluesbreakers played at Launceston's storied *Princess Theatre*, where performers like Olivier, Vivien Leigh, Robert Helpmann and me in Oliver had performed. For some reason I had been roped in to be a 'roadie' in inverted commas. I presume I did this without perpetrating any disasters, because I have no recollection of any of it. I also got to see the show for free and don't recollect that either. After the gig, I do remember that I noticed an old bloke with a ponytail talking to someone. The 'old' bloke was a forty-five-year-old Mayall. How a band as, excuse my French, fucking shit hot as his, playing songs like 'Hideaway' had left me cold is a mystery.)

6

I did have a head start though when it came to testing the waters with a hell of a lot of music. Throughout 1978 and 1979 I worked at a local radio station on night shifts, (punctuated now and then by punishing early mornings which began at 6 am.) On Saturday nights I was employed (alone, although friends and co-workers would visit) to mind a large computer which was programmed to play songs and ads from 6 pm to 1 am. The songs were decanted from vinyl onto large tape spools, while the ads shouted their dumb entreaties from cartridges inside a rotating wheel like an old slide projector. If something went wrong there was a built-in keyboard on which I was able to reset and rejig and generally get everything back in sync. The whole deal was a breeze at the time – it all seems quite complicated now – and I was able to more or less ignore what was actually going to air (as long as it wasn't nothing at all – dead air it would last for five seconds and then the computer would automatically play *something*) in order to listen to records, or steal the ones which had been delivered by record company reps, only to be filed and never passed on to DJs. Coincidentally, most of what Radio 7LA would never play, was what I really liked.

We used to have competitions too, to see who could throw a tea bag from the lunch room onto the awning of the shop opposite. This went on for some time until there was a complaint. We didn't have a leg to stand on and were given a final warning. But then, if you pay with peanuts … considering the chimney-sweep wage we were being paid, finding replacements for the lot of us wouldn't have been a simple task.

The most captivating and eternally evocative song of 1979 was 'Wuthering Heights'. I think most people reacted as I did on first being exposed to it: What … the … fuck … is … this? Whenever

I hear it, I'm catapulted back to 7LA. The best days of my life. EMI – oh here they go again – didn't think 'Wuthering Heights' was a good choice for a single. Kate put her foot down. It was a brave and unique record and would be followed by many more excursions into a territory Kate Bush made completely her own. It's worth mentioning that a solo female performer who was in no sense molded to suit, who celebrated sensuality without having to show any flesh was unique.

If anyone challenged me to cry on cue all I'd need to do would be conjure up the image of Kate Bush at the end of the last date of her first tour. As the spectral lead break takes hold, Bush glides like a wraith to the top of a stage ramp, first waving like a willow in a storm in time with the music, and then leaping up and down with pure joy as the crowd goes nuts. She wasn't everyone's cup of tea, and I had a girlfriend who would have burned her ears off with a blowtorch rather than listen to Kate Bush. It depended really on how much theatre you wanted in your music. For me, Bush stayed on the right side of the pop/prog-rock divide. She was one of a kind and always will be.

When I was sixteen, I was subject to an epiphany even more powerful than hearing The Beatles or the Sex Pistols for the first time. An American band I had heard of, and was curious about, were featured on Countdown, with a syndicated live clip from a US TV show. The band was Cheap Trick, the song was 'Southern Girls' and it blew my head off.

Here was a group apparently created specifically by some cosmic intelligence, for me. They were Power Pop (sort of) New Wave (kind of) hard rock (in a way) and they looked incredible. There were no beards, (just a moustache on the drummer who resembled a slightly overweight accountant) no satin, no capes or kimonos or perms, or keyboards. No extraneous backing singers or bald patches. Okay, the guitarist was bald but he wore an unfashionable goofy baseball hat, and a cardigan, and a bow tie, and drainpipe pants and Black Tiger running shoes. He buzzed around the stage like a wasp on speed, gurning and spitting plectrums, and he played a Gibson Explorer which was the coolest guitar ever. It was the vocalist however who really took my breath away. The white suit, white shirt and golden long hair. The *voice* for god's sake. In order to even out the 'two weirdos' schtick, the bass player was also crazily handsome and also shooshed his hair a lot. Nothing they wore was *tight*. They weren't doing the 'look at my package' thing. The band had a backline of trashed speaker boxes full of lights which was probably a comment on bands who had more Marshalls onstage than Spinal Tap.

Within three minutes I'd been converted. Like meeting a new friend who you have everything in common with. Like love, lust, infatuation and a killer record collection.

Cheap Trick's image wasn't entirely organic; their rejection of the way a rock band should look was based on a determination to look nothing like any rock band ever had. There was clearly a choice to be made about who would play who (and I don't mean who would play *what*.) With his receding hairline and cartoonish stage capers, it was not much of a leap for guitarist Rick Nielsen to up the ante and don clothes he may have found in a skip or at a Salvos. Drummer Bun E Carlos would have been a travesty as a long-haired rock drummer – there *are* photos – so he made himself look as ordinary as possible, which for a rock drummer was very strange to see. Like a supernumerary job-seeker at an accountant firm. All that was required of vocalist Robin Zander was that he choose some sharp suits which folks like Robert Plant and Steven Tyler would clearly eschew (due to the absence of testicular visibility) and look impossibly beautiful. That meant a ban on denim too as well as soft-rock flares, or ripped up punk Levi's. Bass player and brunette Tom Petersson offset Zander, with his gleaming curly hair and chiselled face and together they created the most formidable girl-bait duo since Lennon and McCartney.

I could see how the band could share bills with Kiss and Aerosmith and AC/DC, as well as Elvis Costello and Graham Parker. The term no-wave often means no-good, but Cheap Trick couldn't be categorised. (At that time the only other band who seemed to fit nowhere were The Runaways, but Kim Fowley had designed them as a sexploitation girl-group which tarnished things a tad.) Like all great bands there was an element of burglary at play, some magpie behaviour with Cheap Trick, but nothing any critics were really able to pin on them. The power chords were sometime reminiscent of the Who (as was Carlos's limber drumming), the tunes you might compare to The Beatles, and Zander especially could pull out the Lennon-esque primal scream, but who wasn't compared to The Beatles? The band often dropped hints about other bands in song titles as well. They name-checked The Yardbirds and The Move in interviews, but those bands were more inspirations to get on with it themselves and create something new. Rick Nielsen and Tom Petersson had gone to England in 1967 to absorb the music. In America it was the paisley summer of love but in England the Small Faces, The Animals, The Kinks and Manfred Mann were delivering a raw, and realistic rock'n'roll. Any concessions to psychedelia by, for example, The Stones on *Their Satanic Majesty's Request* were viewed with scepticism and were generally short-lived experiments.

It was my quest now to scour for Cheap Trick records. They were still under the radar in Australia, so it was the record club that came to my rescue in acquiring Cheap Trick albums. The first LP I bought was *In Color* (their second) and the second I bought was self-titled (their first) and surprisingly the third I bought was their third, *Heaven Tonight* (from Wills Record Bar.) At the time, I had to greedily wait for more. The triumvirate of LPs I owned were simply perfect. With 'Surrender', which opened *Heaven Tonight* the band seemed to have reached an apex of pop perfection, you wondered how they could top it. They didn't – not really – but they came close.

Cheap Trick At Budokan catapulted the band into the mainstream. The palpable atmosphere of hysteria – that jet engine squeal that only a stadium full of teenage girls can create – did the trick for Trick. The band had already recorded their fourth studio album, *Dream Police*, before *Budokan* was even considered for a US/Australian release, so the studio album was kept on the backburner for most of 1979. In Japan Cheap Trick were creating a kind of madness amongst their fans that had not been seen since the Beatles. They needed decoys, they had to slip out the back door of hotels covering their heads. It all seemed part of an alluring narrative that I loved. They were on the cover of Rolling Stone. And RAM.

Dream Police is a great record but is also possessed of a slight production sheen that was to become more prominent on the next LP, and thereafter for some time. The cover also broke the tradition of the dreamboats being on the front and the nerds on the back. The whole thing was a set up and looked a bit tacky considering the effort from the art direction department that presumably went into it. (The band decked out in white *Dream Police* faux-cop uniforms.)

I'm able, if it could ever interest you, which it wouldn't, to dissect every Cheap Trick LP between 1980 and 2021. Suffice to say, most of them are not very good. After *Dream Police* the band enlisted George Martin (why?) to produce their album *All Shook Up*. There were maybe three good tunes on it, and it was bombastic, over-cooked, and a kind of self-parody.

They had a number two hit in 1982 ('If You Want My Love' While My Guitar Gently Weeps') and a number one in 1988 (A Really Bad Committee-Written Song Called 'The Flame') Navigate your way through the many Cheap Trick albums and you'll find terrific songs here and there. Either those songs are anomalies, or the band swathed them in crap through laziness. I'm not convinced that Cheap Trick know a good Cheap Trick song when they hear one. Recently the group have begun shifting and shuffling their live set-list to include vintage gems, so ultimately, for their constant commitment to playing 200 shows a year, and in spite of their misdemeanours, you still have to love Cheap Trick.

7

The fashion in Launceston, in terms of what most folks in their twenties listened to, or played in their bands in the late '70s was the stuff I didn't so much not care for as outright despised. Van Morrison, JJ Cale, Dylan, Boz Scaggs, Seals and Crofts, The Doobie Brothers. Being all grown-up now I can see the attraction of 'Brown Eyed Girl', 'Cocaine', many, many Dylan songs, and 'Long Train Running', but I'm not sure I'd feel it necessary to sit down and try to 'get into' *Astral Weeks*. I did buy *Blood On The Tracks*, and, like the usual half-a-fan, a Dylan compilation (Judas!) after I'd seen the documentary *Don't Look Back* in which Dylan's obtuse personality is in full view, to humorous effect (but also to the unhappy chagrin of the overly-solicitous Joan Baez) Dylan was a dude. I liked him.

The intention from the start, when I decided I'd give this band thing a proper crack, was to fight against the prevailing tide of 'yacht rock' in Launceston no matter how amateurish the results. And amateurish they were.

I knew enough chords now to pick out the 'rhythm' guitar parts of most tunes as long as they didn't drift off into Suspended4thDiminished7th territory. (Remember there were no internet cheat sheets in those days.) My skills were rudimentary at best, but I realised that even if I was technically not exactly a virtuoso, I had a fairly good ear for the tricks a lot of acts employed in their chord sequences.

I'd learnt the guitar basics in Grade 10 in the guitar room during music-prac. There were about four of us and we'd make up blues songs ('I Left My Baby Standing In The Rain On Platform 5 At The Railway Station'.) One guy had been having lessons for years so he was default band leader. For the next few years, I'd fiddle with Martin's guitars, so the school assembly song wasn't too challenging. After my HSC I started looking for similarly anti-MOR people to jam with.

Lenny Rainbow (not his real name … he may have not had a real name) ran a secondhand punk paraphernalia shop just outside the CBD in Launceston. He sold badges and military coats and trashed jackets, and more stupidly, swastika flags, but he was too dumb, and I was too dumb to realise that something was wrong there. Neither of us had any neo-Nazi sympathies but the red flags didn't really raise any red flags. In the heady days of punk, shock tactics were the way to go. (Siouxsie Sioux used to wear a swastika arm band and Sid Vicious had a swastika T Shirt, but Sid was so dim it's barely worth commenting on that, and Siouxsie's *faux pas* became apparent when she was on the infamous Grundy/Sex Pistols program, so why didn't *that* cause the great unwashed to jam their switchboards, rather than someone saying 'Fucker'?)

So, at the end of 1979 I picked up the bass again – the instrument was more or less given to me by Spike the punk, who was still failing to grasp the most basic logistical challenges of playing it – and with my older brother Martin, and Lenny, I formed a band.

Martin had learnt classical guitar. He was competent and able to pull out licks that I still can't get my fingers around, but he lacked the kind of attitude and aggression which may have suited us. He was just far too peaceful and placid a person. Lenny somehow found a drumkit which he may have pilfered piece by piece, but he was actually pretty good in an animal-from-the-Muppets way.

We played Buzzcocks, Jam, Radio Birdman, Stooges and Clash covers in the warehouse behind Lenny's shop, Lipstick. He had (somehow, and probably against the landlord's wishes) painted the place, and stenciled onto the walls the insignias of a number of punk bands. The milieu was perfect but the music wasn't.

Even then another bass player who had been in a fairly accomplished punk band called The Specks, and was unemployed after the main songwriter had moved to Sydney, offered to play for us. Idiotically I told Tony that I appreciated the offer but I was the bass player. This hubris was to come back and bite me now and then, although part of it was that the bass was something to hold and I felt less self-conscious than I would have as 'front-man'. Clearly Tony had also looked at the band, heard my bass-playing, and decided to help. It still bothers me that I said no. If for no other reason than he already *looked* right – like he'd stepped out of The Jam.

The warehouse at Lipstick was perfectly suited as a club, and Lenny held a few punk-themed nights there featuring the 'other' punk band in town, Pillsey and the Pushrods, who were from King Island. I imagine the only place quieter and more dull musically than Launceston, would be King Island. But they could rip it up. The punk gigs ended when Lenny's brother Garnett burned the place (presumably by accident) to the ground. It would be another lean year for my musical career.

1980 was an awful time. I had found myself in a relationship which didn't provide the kind of romantic thrills I had been waiting for. I caught, from this blameless girl, glandular fever, and was laid low for a month or so. I was still studying but at a college without any of the social benefits of Launceston Matric. No quadrangle in which to share gossip on sunny days. No flirting. Now it was lectures at 7.30 pm, and hauntingly empty hallways.

Eventually I had a nervous breakdown, dropped out, and spent the second half of the year modifying my new medication until I had my head above water again. What seemed to be the end of everything was really a blip which enabled me to get away from studying and instead play with my slot car set.

The new music was still powerful and questing, and the bands were exploring new territory. The second wave of post-punk was spearheaded by the now monstrously popular The Jam and was about to mutate towards synth-pop, post-punk, goth, the New Romantic movement, the two-tone ska revival, the very beginnings of indie rock, and more. Funk and disco were gathering pace and synthesizers were on the rise courtesy of Orchestral Manoeuvres In The Dark, Soft Cell, John Foxx and The Human League. The Cure were pushing through their formidably chilly, almost nihilistic singles period. The best LP of the year though was Squeeze's *Argy Bargy*, brimming with exceptional tunes, kitchen sink dramas and confident arrangements.

Joy Division scared the absolute shit out of me. Ian Curtis was dead when *Closer* was released. I found it impossible (in my fragile mental state) to even *try* to listen to it. The record (when I finally summoned the courage to give it a spin) was chilling in all senses of the word. Curtis doesn't so much sing as intone. A doomsayer sending echoes of a broken soul from a room without light.

After Curtis's suicide Joy Division morphed into New Order, bought some extra drums bits and a synth and (with one ear on the new direction of Sparks) wrote the gloomy but dancefloor friendly (Blue Monday.)

The old guard hung on tenaciously, becoming less and less relevant by the day and mostly ignore by the press. To say that Yes were your favourite band was to admit to being old, no matter what your age. Namedropping Pink Floyd would cause sniggers. And quite rightly too. Dig the new breed.

8

Over the summer of 1980-1981 I had friends who were renting and living in a large house just out of town. Everyone called it Frederick St for obvious reasons. The backyard was massive. (I know. I mowed the lawn one day as a thank you for all the goon-bag wine I'd been plied with when I visited.) It was time to start jamming again. Martin and I again, this time with a new drummer called Kevin. Kevin was a bit of a grifter and spiv, with no history he wanted to divulge. He just appeared. Without tuition and if I remember, without having tried it before, he was instantly pretty good.

We played outside in the sun and we were still mostly relying on Buzzcocks and early Cure songs, now augmented by The Undertones. The Undertones were an inspiration. They looked like their Mums had dressed them. Knitted jumpers, ankle-freezer denims, boots, unfashionable chainsaw haircuts. They hailed from the war zones of Northern Ireland but unlike the foghorn politics of U2 wrote songs about table soccer, Mars Bars and ambulances, as well as girls of course, most notably on the bona fide classic 'Teenage Kicks'.

When legendary English DJ John Peel heard 'Teenage Kicks' he called it "the greatest song in history" and played it three times in a row. Thereafter he opened his show with the song until his untimely death.

(This dispelled the feeling I had that if I wrote songs, they should be about 'politics' – from the monarchy, to crooked cops, to Irish independence, to smalltown tedium. I could just write about girls.)

In 1993 I sent John Peel a copy of the first Lust In Space album with a letter suggesting that, since the record had been recorded in Launceston, which was about as far away from London as you could get, he might think about playing a song.

So he did. John Peel. I didn't hear it – the BBC didn't make it as far as Melbourne where I was – but a number of people in Asia did hear it and left messages to say as much. I'm sure that the line "*I dig the Undertones*" must have helped. I still get a kick out of the idea that John Peel said, "I've never played music from Tasmania before."

The prickly Feargal Sharkey left the Undertones, put on a nice suit, and had a few hits with songs like 'A Good Heart'. The Undertones had evolved into a more subtle outfit. We did cover a song called 'Wednesday Week' from their third album but the naivete which had attracted me in the first place had been supplanted, I suppose to represent their gathering years. (They were now 22 years old or something ridiculous.)

We still played Radio Birdman's cut and paste version of the *Hawaii Five-O* theme song 'Aloha Steve and Danno'. The song tended to highlight the fact that Martin could hit all the right notes, but not with the fire and brimstone of Wayne Kramer, Chris Masuak, Denis Tek or any number of hard rock axe heroes.

These get togethers were somewhere between cottage industry gigs – there were always people at the house – and practices. At night, with our girlfriends, we'd steal gnomes, and concrete flamingos and leave ransom notes, and then hide them in the shed at Frederick St. When a cop arrived one day to tell us to shut up with the bad music, he stood next to the shed without looking through the window at the stash of garden ornaments. It was a tense moment but ultimately hilarious.

I eventually secured a job I liked at Myer, in the display department. This meant I helped with odd tasks on every floor, so there was plenty of variety. Three of us were charged with creating a carriage for Cinderella for the Launceston Christmas Parade. It was a *papier mache* fiasco, made worse when the display boss looked at the wooden framework we'd added to an actual vintage carriage, and smashed it to pieces.

None of this is relevant of course except for the fact that the radio was hammering the new John Lennon single 'Starting Over'. So my memories of Myer are based around the taste of Banana Big M, a gorgeous girl who worked at Myer called Kate … and John Lennon. Then John Lennon was shot. I'd just got home and Mum rang from her work, which was the local newspaper. Initially my thoughts were something like, 'Oh … that's bad I guess.' It wasn't until the TV news reports began piling up that I responded with an appropriate emotional surge. This sense of sorrow was only compounded by the fact that 'Shaddup You Face' was now sitting on top of the charts. Life went on.

Myer sacked me for being on antidepressants. I don't think I'd have stood for that if I wasn't so young and naive.

9

The band was now known as Anxiety State and played its first 'proper' gig if you like at a kind of game arcade. The games, which would now be considered vintage – Space Invaders, Galaga, Frogger – were cutting edge at the time and would now be precious antiques. From memory we weren't too bad, but my recall is actually pretty vague and fractured. I think I wanted to get it over with so I could have sex with my girlfriend. Leave me alone I was only eighteen.

Next up was The Launceston Regatta – one of those agricultural shows, with not so much agriculture, but plenty of rowing, fairy floss and fireworks. And in 1981, a rock concert too. We were booked along with our friends Lipstik (as their support.) They were seriously good. Their vocalist Sharon (now married to "proggy" Graham) was stylish, confident and had a voice to match. Their covers were much better thought-out than ours too. (Whenever we supported them, I used to think – and want to announce – "It's ok … there's a PROPER band on after us.")

With all our friends present as well as a decent crowd of the curious, Anxiety State managed to get by. Periodically I'd stare down at the crowd to ensure they weren't laughing at us. This was a fairly feeble barometer of our capabilities and professionalism but the positive crowd reaction actually fulfilled my requirements – which was 'survival at all costs'.

By this time we had a second guitarist. Frank was a blues fan and also had a fondness for interesting bands like T Rex, Cockney Rebel, and The Yardbirds. Our set list was altered to accommodate Frank's tastes. But Frank was also spruiking songs to us by Robert Johnson, John Lee Hooker, Muddy Waters and Hendrix, and even though he educated me about swamp and Chicago blues, our attempts to play songs like

'Redhouse' were less than successful. We found common ground in Australian punk, Thin Lizzy and the Church. Frank dressed well. He had leather Beatles boots, black drainpipes, white shirts and sparkly blue waistcoats. His hair was very long. He looked the part, but often couldn't necessarily play the parts. A lovely guy in any case.

Our new drummer, George was a friend from the soccer club. To be brutally frank, it was Frank who was the better 'get' than George, who could just about keep a beat, even if it wasn't the beat we needed. He was a good guy though, and funny, in spite of him telling taller tales than the Chrysler Building. George also suffered from blisters at the few gigs we played, which necessitated at times an early finish.

About those gigs; one was a 'social' at the school where Dad taught (and where he had organised a practice room for us.) It was a successful night, and for the first time I was approached by girls – I was eighteen and they were fifteen – for whom a boy in a band with blonde hair was something quite exotic. Graham (now into Japan, the band) had bought a Prophet 5 Synthesizer and even though he couldn't even play (chopsticks), joined the band for the gig, in order to colour certain songs with a variety of sound effects. He also applied make-up to heighten whatever effect he was aiming at. I have no idea if the noises he was making were a help or hindrance. The gig was at the gymnasium which meant we had a vast "changeroom" too. Dream on you other bands … ha!

Our setlist, due to a combination of mistaken ambition and wanting to seem more 'with it', was now an unholy combination of blues songs, Thin Lizzy songs (a band all of us could agree we enjoyed), punk, but more the deep cuts such as 'Somebody's Watching Me' by the Boys Next Door, and covers of covers like a cover of Japan's terrible cover of 'Don't Rain On My Parade', by Barbra Streisand (from *Funny Girl*.) I'm not sure how that song made the cut because by early 1982 we had learned one-hundred-and-three other songs and could surely have picked twenty worth sticking to.

I was on the social committee of the soccer club so there were also a few shows for the club to raise money, at a community hall, where we had a large stage, and trestle tables were erected for players, male and female, to collect and empty plastic cups of beer, over and over, until they were sick. One social was shut down, and I mean the plug was literally pulled, by the custodians of the premises. With booze secreted any place anyone could hide it, the drinking continued unabated in the bushes behind the hall. The next time we tried to play at the hall with less dramas, quite the opposite happened. Martin and Dad had built a 'pre-amp' for Martin's homemade speaker cabinet. It was only small – about the size of a loaf of bread – and looked like something from a spaceship in a bad '50s SF movie. Anyway, the thing overheated and started to smoke, then it sparked a bit and caught fire. I was concentrating on singing and didn't notice. Martin thought something was wrong with his guitar, so it took him some time to notice as well. George was first to stop playing, which made the rest of us turn around to be faced with a small ball of flames, and acrid black smoke. There were no sprinklers (thankfully) so we cut the power, knocked the amp to the floor and jumped up and down on it until it was a) completely destroyed, and b) no longer on fire. Martin's speaker box was smoking a little too, having been singed quite badly. I poured a beer on it and then it was okay. We jerry-rigged a lead through the PA, to create an amp and carried on as if nothing had happened.

My work life had been chequered. I used to go to interviews sometimes and flub them deliberately in order to retain the dole. If I was asked where I saw myself in two years-time, I'd reply "I'm not fussed as long as there's a good tape in the car." This was a job-killer, but it was also true.

I auditioned for a position presenting the weather at the local

TV station. The audition was a fiasco … but they gave me the job anyway. Even though I wandered tele-visually into people's homes three nights a week, the workload was only three hours or so a week. Not long after this I became a salesperson for a stationery company. I guess I enjoyed it. Looking back, it was certainly more enjoyable in retrospect than I may have realised at the time. One full-time job was enough, so I scuttled the weather gig. I was tired of idiots asking me what the weather was going to be like if I was out shopping or in a bar. So I left TV behind. Had I been gifted with any common sense, I would have used the weather position as a springboard for other jobs in broadcasting, but nope, I was eighteen and I knew best.

The mixtape was every teenager's mutually rewarding send-and-return method of listening to new music. It was up to the recorder to highlight the best tunes of their recent vinyl purchases with a curated cassette. And in a scratch-my-back deal, the given would become giver. I still have all the mixtapes which Graham knocked up for me, but own a car now which horrifyingly doesn't feature a tape player.

The mixtape was a crucial part of the new job for me. I used to drive to the various satellite towns and hamlets that surrounded Launceston to collect orders, and the tapes' contents are now completely infused into my emotional memory.

After eighteen months or so with Frank in the fold we were booked – oh, by the way, we were now called Another Script – by a soccer guy to play a function for a barbecue at the local Italian Club.

Frank had a sister called Diane. She was etiolated to the extent that the word 'ghostly' barely does her justice. She was the least robust or vigorous human being I ever met, and she also seemed to be Frank's default complaints department.

After the gig which was variously diabolical, amateurish, and finally just about competent, (although the pair of brothers who were behind the mixing desk were the Abbott and Costello of sound engineering) it was decided (by Diane) that Frank had now left the band. Frank was … well, circumspect. But he did leave.

My depression became serious again in the middle of the year and I had to leave my job. Playing music was always a way of staying busy and continued to be so, pretty much for all my life. (This is not a book about 'that stuff', so let's not dwell on it.)

The band re-convened with Andrew (you remember him from the college assembly) playing guitar. This version of the group was actually pretty good. Andrew and Martin were able to swap Thin Lizzy twin-guitar parts with little effort. The best of these tunes was 'Waiting For An Alibi' which wasn't exactly a piece of cake to nail down.

We played another college social, this time for sixteen-to-eighteen-year-olds, and we were good. Actually properly good. Our main issue was the genre-swapping setlist. The Cure, then Duran Duran, then Chuck Berry, then Bowie. The easiest way to overcome this problem was to replace the covers with originals. But none of us was any good at writing. Martin and I certainly got proficient in this area, but not for at least three years. Why we bothered with a song as profoundly average as 'Hungry Like The Wolf' by Duran Duran can only be explained by the effect that that band were having on fashion, more than music. Andrew and I in particular fancied the whole New-Romantic style thing, and I looked enough like Duran Duran's bass player John Taylor to get the occasional comment.

It has to be said too, that 1982 wasn't exactly a festival of great records. Not for my liking anyway. As an example, the Jam released *The Gift*, which ('Town Called Malice' notwithstanding) was a bit ropey. Squeeze released *Sweets From A Stranger* which ('Black Coffee In Bed' notwithstanding) was also pretty ropey. You get the idea. NME voted 'The Look Of Love' by ABC as the fourth best single of the year. The tumbleweeds were rolling across the parched cadaver of pop.

In Australia it was the year of Men at Work. *Business As Usual* was a canny record but not one you'd actually play. The yanks fell for the Aussie schtick, as did a hell of a lot of Aussies. I can't bring myself to mention the lead single. You know very well what it was. The album just pipped the somnolent soundtrack to *Chariots Of Fire* in the end of year charts.

10

Another Script were largely diminished when Andrew moved to Melbourne. Lipstik once again had us support them, this time at a party on a farm about 40 kms from town. The gig was fine, I think, but I was by then on such mammoth doses of antidepressants, that I'd already had several seizures and was tempting fate getting up to sing at all.

In keeping with the whole cheap fireworks, cheaper wine, vibe of the evening I got pretty drunk, and had hardly any sleep before the owners of the property started "soo-ee"-ing everyone off their land. I had opened the door of my car, ready to drive home, when I hit the ground like a sack of fertiliser. I'm not sure how long I was out for but have no memory of the gigs.

It was time to end this chemical zombification, and for the band in turn to find a new second guitarist.

The best thing I can say about Rowan was that he was one of the funniest people I've ever met. And believe me I've hung out with some sharp wits. Nothing about Rowan was very rock'n'roll though. Frank and Andrew looked like they should be in bands. Rowan wasn't daggy, or a redneck, but he just put a warm jumper on, stood in one place, and strummed his guitar. From memory, there really wasn't much reason for Rowan actually being in the band. His technique was to sort of 'play along' with songs adding neither light nor shade nor any audible contribution.

For the entirety of 1983 this was what Rowan did … however, he did make road trips more enjoyable, and practice was funnier.

This was the year when we stretched our wings, filled the petrol tanks, and began playing out in the country. The pub in a small town is a hub, and doesn't really need a band in it to fill any sort of musical or entertainment void, which, if there is a jukebox, there won't be. And yet we were booked, often, to do our thing in the pubs of St Marys, Scottsdale and Longford. We did have a kind of agent, who booked a bunch of bands, but he wouldn't have been making anything from us. At that time though, any gig was a good gig, and now and then these gigs *were* good gigs.

I have fond memories of some of these overnight stays. The accommodation at St Marys had a whiff of 'Call The Midwife' about it. Musky mattresses, smeary windows, motheaten carpet. But we were furnished with a full breakfast and nothing could be better than that to get your engine restarted after only a few hours sleep.

It would be disingenuous to claim that these places couldn't be a little rough from time to time. At Longford one night the entire population of the lounge bar drifted outside to watch 'the fights' – noted in my diary as though they could be predicted by your watch. One ploy to ensure you never got tangled up in the troubles was to find the chap who seemed nominally to be the alpha-male at the pub, and either get to know him, or have him come up and sing 'Wild Thing.'

One night at the coastal town of Bridport, I smoked a fair chunk of a buddha stick, and spent a least two songs crawling around the stage looking for my plectrum. Moments of unprofessionalism like this didn't seem to faze the audience.

I had moved out of home for the first time and was now living with Rowan and our friend Matthew who was the band's roadie/lighting guy. (Our sound person, Marshall was a kid-savant, about eighteen years old and already building his own mixing desks and amps. When we played larger rooms, Marshall was able, by his magic powers, to apply a number of spectral effects to make us sound better than we really were.)

Our flat which was above shops in the CBD became a drop-in centre, much as Fredrick St had been in years past. Sometime our 'groupies' (and to be honest they kinda were just that) would pop-in and cook breakfast, or clean-up the place which was very kind of them. I've never been able to decide if someone friendly who goes to every gig might see some sort of cachet in hanging out. I do recall one girl walking through town with me and muttering something about being with a local rock star. It wasn't so much that she'd said it, as the fact that I clearly was about as miniscule a rock star as you could imagine, even in Launceston. There was never any sexual aspect to these devoted slightly lopsided friendships, and I don't think that was the aim of the girls.

The gigs increased in number and the venues and events became more impressive, in our eyes at least. We began doing supports at the main nightclub in town, Rock Central, and the agency (which was going through a lean patch for available acts) booked us to play larger socials at larger colleges. We travelled to Hobart to support a band called The Shifters who were a well-honed, finely tuned and brutally powerful hard rock act. It wasn't entirely my cup of tea but it was impossible not to be impressed by their musicianship and showmanship. It was an education for me.

Then George left. He told us he couldn't keep up the payments on his drumkit, which may or may not have been true. In a domino effect, Rowan then left, and the reasons for that are as mysterious now as they were then. Essentially that was the end of Another Script, Mk 1.

After a hiatus of six months or so, Martin and I reconvened with a new drummer, Tim. He was fifteen and could play the drums like a demon. The only impediment was that he and Martin were both in another band now, a five piece with a hotshot lead guitarist. It was nice to get Another Script up and running again but we would be condemned I felt, to supporting the other band indefinitely.

To my surprise Strange Bedfellows, the *other* band, fell apart, so Tim and Martin could now concentrate on Another Script, and Another Script could concentrate on getting better.

By now we had three or four of our own songs, none of

which I would ever want you to hear. One of the problems was the ongoing eclecticism not only of the covers but also the originals. I was influenced by the shouty anthems of U2, the churchy grandeur of Echo And The Bunnymen and the glammy silliness of The Glitter Band. That might sound interesting, but the songs weren't really interesting, believe me.

Then the Violent Femmes appeared. My first exposure to the band was on a late-night music show called *Rock Arena*, which was for grown ups and presented with the formality of the evening news by the fragile but trustworthy Suzanne Dowling. The song was 'Gone Daddy Gone' and it was highlighted by an off-kilter xylophone solo which made my jaw drop. It wouldn't have been unusual for us to throw a Femmes cover into the set. None of it was logical to start with, and 'Blister In The Sun', in my eyes was begging to be included.

The Femmes seemed to have no antecedents apart from their vague resemblance to the minimalism of the Velvet Underground or Modern Lovers. Brian Ritchie, who is now an arts luminary in Tasmania, was the best bass player I had ever heard, skittering up and down the neck of his acoustic bass like a dervish. Later on, in part-time bands formed for a bit of fun, I would play quite a few Femmes songs in the set. After all there was no logical connection between the songs we played anyway, but never did I consider or hope to play the way Ritchie did.

When I made one of my customary visits to my (very straight-laced) friend Darren, who ran a music shop in town, I enthused over the Violent Femmes and I can still recall the look of disdain on his face. So they were doing something right. Darren's own popular covers band were nothing short of horrific.

The central and more or less only club for live music by 1984 was Night Moves. We were quite realistic about our abilities to entertain two hundred people who were far more interested in having a drink and a dance to the disco tunes than seeing a band playing weirdo music and we never expected to headline on the weekends.

The guy who ran the place was good to us – we headlined Thursdays, with supports now and then on Fridays and Saturdays. Finding another guitarist would have been relatively easy and eminently sensible. The sound was a bit thin, in spite of Marshall's best efforts. We didn't even countenance searching for another guitarist. In fact Rowan asked to be re-instated and I said no. If we'd wanted to embrace something modern, and in some ways conventionally suited to the era, a keyboardist would have been a better bet. That never occurred to me.

In a major step up we inveigled ourselves onto the bill of a two day "festival" which featured in order of name-dropping; Divinyls, Eurogliders, Rose Tattoo, Uncanny X Men, Dynamic Hepnotics, Allniters, The Runners and some local acts. We were on early and managed to have our photo on the front of the evening paper (remember those?) Andrew had come over from Melbourne to play bass at the concert (allowing me to have two free arms which I didn't really know what to do with). We'd also given him the call up because we were booked to record three of our songs the following weekend with the view to releasing a single.

After we'd played the outdoor gig, and because it was all new to us, we wandered around backstage star-spotting between bands. I was especially impressed with Uncanny X Men – a strange band to be impressed by. Rather than being the tight-trousered bogan I later realised he was, Brian Mannix appeared to be hilarious, and the pop-rock songs which revealed themselves in time to be remarkably flimsy, sounded really catchy. Later in the day I bailed up a man who, because of his blonde mullet, I presumed to be an X Man, and gushed in great washes of cringe about how much I'd enjoyed their set. Unfortunately I was talking to a guy from The Runners. To make things worse, The Runners were a dreadful band.

Later that night we took to the stage at Night Moves where pretty much every band from the big city was present to relax and have a drink. The place was full and it appeared to be a perfect opportunity to step up and impress the visitors. "Welcome to Night Moves!" I said. "Welcome to Launceston!" At the end of our first song there was silence, punctuated only by the clink of glasses, and the murmur of quiet conversations at the bar. Nobody took the faintest notice of us.

By now about half the set (if we only played for fifty minutes or so) was original material. Two sets required a deeper dip into the covers at hand. What can I say about my songs? I can say in general that they seemed to be liked well enough. I suppose they sounded a bit like an unholy and ill-begotten marriage of The Church and Elvis Costello. That's a grand comparison for tunes which were never really arranged properly, were sung with little conviction and which had little in common with each other. But they were ours and that in itself was unusual for a Launceston act. The decision to make a record enabled us to pique the interest of the press, and take another step forward in the quest to be not just taken seriously, but to be ahead of the pack.

Not much happens in either of the songs we chose for the 45 (having recorded three at the only studio in the state, in Hobart.) To my ears, if we replicated what we played live, that was pretty much the idea. Hence there were very few overdubs. The finished product was … well, okay, I s'pose. We did choose the wrong songs because the one we shelved was probably the best. We recorded everything in two days, and Marshall mixed the results the following Sunday, with his girlfriend nagging at hm to hurry up, because she wanted to get back home to Launceston.

I designed a suitably amateurish, punkish sleeve, and when the vinyl was delivered, I began dropping six or so copies at each of the handful of record shops in town. Two days later I began getting calls for supplies to be re-stocked. What was this all about? Even now I don't know who was actually buying this curio but buying it people were. After a week or so, the record (on real sales figure) should have been at number two on the Tasmanian charts. The radio programmers in charge of these things decided that this could only be a corollary of all our friends ganging up and buying perhaps not just copies, but multiple copies. I didn't have that many friends and neither did the rest of the band to my knowledge.

We were interviewed on radio, and on a TV rock show, and I think we were played on 2JJ as it was then, but our chart position at home peaked at about No.36. It was a bit insulting really. The Beatles charted in Liverpool when they were otherwise unknown, and I don't think anyone fooled themselves into thinking that there wasn't a provincial popularity angle.

One evening I wandered into a pub and the song was playing on a jukebox. I was with a soccer friend, so he loudly told the room to "Take that rubbish off!" A woman stood up and said, "My daughter chose that." That was the mystery of our first record.

11

By August the three-piece Another Script had played fifty shows. The venue I enjoyed visiting most was The Orient Club in Hobart. A dank, pub dungeon room for the disaffected punks and goths of the South. One night we were supported by Midnight Oil who wanted to warm-up for their stadium show the next night. They borrowed our gear and played for a good hour or so with Tim holding down his drumkit 'traps' (the silver stands that Cymbals are attached to) lest Rob Hirst send them flying across the venue. Being too young to drink, and in fact too young to even be in the place, the bottle of Scotch that Hirst bought Tim wasn't really an age-appropriate gift. So I took it off his hands.

We were making good money. The Orient Club could only afford to pay us $150, but remember this was a small venue in 1984. Other larger venues in Hobart paid us $450 and plied us with Scotch too, and included a few rooms upstairs to sweeten the deal. We played a large hotel called The Downtowner in Hobart one night and were rewarded with … six … hundred … dollars. Sometimes we were on door deals, but none of these were disastrous, and were often buttressed by a 'retainer' of $100. We were big fish in a small pond. The average fee we could ask for was about $250. Added to the dole I was living quite comfortably on one show a week, and often there were two. That sort of money was unheard of in Melbourne, except for the musical elite.

We supported Dragon at the Civic Centre in a North Western town called Burnie (eulogised in a Midnight Oil song). Half way through Dragon's listless set there was a power cut. An agonisingly long one. Marc Hunter proved himself to be not much of a master of ceremonies and the awkwardness was reaching fever pitch, when there was a loud thump and the PA began working again. Tensions appeared to be high within the Dragon camp. The late Paul Hewson decided to take a nap on stage while the roadies were dismantling the stage gear, while Todd Hunter was sitting in the band's Tarago, in mid-winter, wanting nothing more than to get back to their hotel, or back to a different state.

Hopefully their hotel wasn't the Menai, the reputation of which was only superseded by the reality of spending an evening there. Another Script supported the Shifters at The Menai, and it's a good job the Shifters were headlining, because we weren't the kind of band the average Burnie footballer would pay money to see.

The gig was actually not so bad and we met the local 'alternative' folks, members of the groups The Fear Of Dance and Noddy's Revenge who had bravely opened their own venue; the Big Ears club.

Back in our room, Matthew dismantled the TV. I was too much of a goody-goody to wreck a hotel room, and rather than drink Bourbon from a bottle, asked the Shifters entourage if they had any milk, as I felt like a cup of tea.

My friend Ted (The Fear Of Dance) who I met that night avoided a thorough beating one night outside a club in Devonport because word got around that he was Sally Lethborg's brother, and Sally Lethborg was quite high up in the biker community. Ted would have made things worse by giving them lip. (He and I recorded some songs in the 2000s which were probably the best I'd been involved with. Just saying lest I forget.)

Most venues didn't offer accommodation, so that meant driving home in the early hours. The midlands of Tasmania would be frost-covered and the temperature would drop to about -3c. the roads were riddled with black ice and how we managed to avoid trouble over and over again was a miracle. Martin would be exhausted, having already worked a full day as a pathologist, before hotfooting it to Hobart to play. On the way home he'd have to have numerous disco naps, his wakefulness overseen by a nervous Marshall in the passenger seat. (Marshall never did learn how to drive. That's so strange).

Another group I discovered in 1984 was Aztec Camera. Their songwriter/guitarist/vocalist Roddy Frame was younger than me so considering his precocious talents I was always going to feel that I was in his shadow, although comparing myself, or hoping to emulate Roddy Frame was highly unrealistic. I gave the *High Land Hard Rain* album a decent thrashing and still consider it the work of a kind of a modern-day pimply Mozart. As Scottish pop music began to creep into the mainstream via bands like Orange Juice and Josef K, and other releases on the legendary Postcard label, Aztec Camera were spotted and signed to the Anglo-centric American Label Sire (who had also snapped up The Undertones in the late '70s).

Looming ominously over every new act hoping to keep up to speed with the technology and hair gel of the '80s however, were a new band called The Smiths. From the get-go (their first single 'Hand In Glove' was a seismic event, unpredicted and shocking) the group were being coveted by critics and fans.

Their vocalist, Morrissey, an ex-rock writer of little note as well as bedroom depressive and member of the New York Dolls fan club, had formed an alliance with guitarist Johnny Marr, and the rest as they say was history. The androgenous and flamboyant singer, necklaced and with orchids poking out of the back of his Levi's 501s was untutored but a naturally gifted singer. It was The Smiths' lyrics though which were unique. The first line of 'Hand in glove goes, '*Hand in glove / the sun shines out of our behinds.*' The follow up 'This Charming Man' boasts extraordinary wordsmithery; '*Why pamper life's complexities when the leather runs smooth on the bicycle seat?*'

The Smiths dominated not just music, but the culture of the times for the next four years, pushing back against the excesses of the mulleted pop stars, and giving good interview. Morrissey was happy to sound off to anyone who would listen and was suitably quotable, but how is it possible for a pop group to sing a song about the queen which features the lines, '*So I broke into the palace / with a sponge and a rusty spanner / She said "I've seen you and you cannot sing" / I said "That's nothing you should hear me play piano."*'

At a stretch the Smiths sounded a little bit, with their guitar sound, like The Byrds. Recognising that The Smiths could be covered, we duly did so with their song 'What Difference Does it Make?', which in hindsight was possibly the weakest track on The Smiths self-title debut. It would have been more credible for us to cover a Byrds songs rather than 'the new thing', but we did find 'the new things' compelling. (These included Echo And The Bunnymen, U2 and Hoodoo Gurus.)

In the US, another band who had broken through the college radio indie scene into the alternative-mainstream if such a thing existed, were REM. Unlike the Smiths, the vocal delivery verged on 'Mumblecore' so it was never entirely clear what Michael Stipe was saying. ("They're the only band that mutters" said one journo wag.) The Byrds comparisons were more accurate, but there had been a psychedelic revival anyway with bands like The Feelies, The Bangles, and The Long Ryders being collectively part of a scene christened The Paisley Underground. In New Zealand The Chills and The Bats might have been tied into the movement, and locally, the Church. What REM had was an air of mystery and intent, which seemed to invite the listener to dive in further to see what they could find.

12

In October 1984 I moved to Melbourne to share a place with Graham. With a mixture of determination and what seems now to be a long-lost energy, I worked hard to get enough money to pay the rent and have enough left to attend gigs. Initially I was catapulted into the suburbs, door-knocking for a roofing company offering free quotes. You might be surprised how well that went and how many people with adequate roofs were willing to have someone lie to them about their needing another one. I was also invited in for a cup of tea by several lonely elderly ladies, which was sweet, but would leave me sad for them.

I began going to see the bands I'd heard about in Tassie or had read about. Chief amongst the acts I wanted to see were The Huxton Creepers. To say I was disappointed would be to tell the biggest lie in world history, the biggest since Richard Nixon said, I am not a crook. The Creepers were pretty much perfect. A wall of guitars, earworm tunes and front-man Rob Craw oozing confidence, charisma and belting it all out with a voice which I instantly realised was the one I should have been emulating. My own performative skills, which I'd always thought were pretty hot, don't you know, were now put in sharp contrast by a guy who knew what he was doing, fronting a band, who knew what they were doing, playing songs written by a group who in every aspect knew how that was done.

The first time I saw The Huxton Creepers was at The Club on Smith St in Collingwood. For many years it was my favourite venue. A large comfortable downstairs band room, and upstairs bar with music TV and a pool table. It was there that I also saw the Go-Betweens. The Creepers gig was a kind of revelation but the Go-Betweens was a trip into some giddily celestial sensorium of wonder. Honestly. Sometimes you have to be there. I was a fan, but even so this was an unexpected feeling I hadn't had since 1979.

At the so-punk-it-hurts Seaview Ballroom in St Kilda I witnessed the giant rumbling monster that was the Beasts Of Bourbon. There was no 'full house' sign at the Ballroom. You just forced your way in as though boarding a Japanese commuter train.

The band seemed pretty loud, but the PA wasn't working. When the problem was fixed there occurred a wave which threw your body backwards like a missile blast. But it was just the band sounding how they liked to sound. I'd be lifted off my feet and deposited on the other side of the room. Either you surrendered to the experience (I did) or ran for it.

To be honest I was a little overwhelmed in my early days in Melbourne. The alternative crowd seemed larger than life. They seemed to know more than me and had had experiences I hadn't had. While I would enter a venue vibrating with anticipation, my new friends were very ho-hum about the whole thing.

An expat who I had known (I think) from gigs we both went to in Launceston, (Martin Coupe, brother of writer Stuart Coupe) had studied at RMIT where he had a met a group of music fans soon forming a drinking club called the EMUs. One of their number had become The Huxton Creepers manager. Martin introduced me to Mark, and Mark was able to secure a few shows for us. It was all very effortless. Soon I was a kind of honorary member of the EMUs which also boasted the members of Painters and Dockers, a crazed pop-punk band whose gigs usually ended in stage invasions. Their songs had titles like 'The Boy Who Lost His Jocks At Flinders Street Station.' And 'Mohawk Baby'; *She don't live on a reservation / She's not into culture-preservation ooga chugga.* Casual racism wasn't really examined in those days. Kids had mohawks. The Dockers were just mixing the traditional and the modern. You do wonder though if that might be worth a cancellation these days.

Being utterly unpretentious, and in some sense mocking the seriousness of bands like The Birthday Party, Painters And Dockers were able to garner a wide and democratic appeal. This enabled them to play suburban beer barns, and regional areas without their inner-city fanbase feeling they'd sold out. This was a tricky balance which only a few bands (like TISM) could manage.

The kind of unselfconscious stagecraft the band would display – louche, confident, vibrant, even amused – was something I needed to learn about. It helped camouflage the Dockers' lack of musicianship, which was … well, notable. They played to their strengths. Their songs appealed to almost everyone who wasn't the kind of person whose idea of a good time was standing in the rain listening to Leonard Cohen.

Tim and Martin bravely upped and shifted to Melbourne too. I'm not sure what I thought Another Script could achieve now that we were together in the big smoke, but it would certainly be more than the prizes on offer in Tasmania. We rehearsed and now had a setlist centred around our own songs, with covers kept at hand to be slotted in when needed.

Andrew lived in a mansion in Toorak with his girlfriend and her brother, who was a mediocre photographer. God knows who paid the rent, however there were plenty enough rooms to accommodate two more musicians.

Before we'd played in Melbourne we counter-intuitively returned to Tassie at Christmas to play some shows. The most important, perhaps even prestigious (in a small way) of these was the statewide band competition. We placed second from about a dozen hopefuls. The competition was won by Sunshine Ward (nee Lipstick) who were clearly the best, and who, if it wasn't for their jobs in Launceston, could have done well on the mainland. Coming in third was Darren the guitar shop guy's band. Third. Ha ha ha. The other bands were interesting and original enough but simply too untutored and sloppy to bother the judges.

On New Year's Eve we headlined Night Moves in Launceston, and threw in some songs like Jailbreak (the AC/DC one) Roadhouse Blues, Gary Glitter's Rock'n'Roll, – no-one at that time knew what Gary Glitter had been up to – The Everly Brothers' 'The Price of Love' and 'Wild Thing' to keep the dancefloor populated. Artistic expression be damned.

Back in Melbourne Martin and Mark, the promoter, conspired to get us a gig at the Seaview (or Crystal) Ballroom, the birthplace of punk in Melbourne. And the venue du jour for bands like The Birthday Party, Models, Whirliwirld, Crime and The City Solution and X as well as visitors like XTC and Magazine. We supported a band called The Wreckery who were heavily influenced by the *sturm und drang* of The Birthday Party and were colloquially known by some as The Smackery for obvious reasons.

The ballroom was part of a group of venues which constituted the stop-offs of what was known as the 'Fitzroy St crawl', which would begin at The Ballroom and proceed to The Prince of Wales and beyond. All the bars were suitably grungy and populated by grifters, chancers, drug addicts, sex workers, journos, bands, the homeless, the bewildered, the drunk and the denizens of art schools and Unis.

There were no dark hotspots on Fitzroy St. Anything nefarious occurred in the backstreets and it was actually an entirely safe and friendly place to be. Later on, two major venues opened and the Ballroom closed. At around the same time the formerly rock'n'roll heavy Prince Of Wales stopped most of their gigs and concentrated on dance parties. By the late '80s Touring rock acts usually played at the purpose built and characterless Palace, with sit down shows occurring next door (and next to Luna Park) at the Palais, a beautiful art-deco gem built in the twenties.

Back in early 1985 with Another Script accepting anything we could get after a not-awful start at the Ballroom, we played at a venue in Richmond called The Tiger Lounge. This place was a little way off the regular band strips, and having no following, and from memory no headliner on the night, we stiffed. I remember a friend of mine being there, and no-one else.

By now we only had a few covers in the set. 'He's A Whore' by Cheap Trick and 'Goodbye My Love' by The Glitter Band which I'd partially ripped off for one of my songs anyway. The last Another Script gig happened at the Prince of Wales that May, Tim and Martin found the whole thing a bit of a drain on their various resources and both moved home.

What the band needed, and always needed was a creative leader to take the onus off me. I did my best but my songs were the kind you'd normally find on a B Side. Someone ambitious with charisma and some inarguable talent and an unquenchable ego is the spotlit figure that most bands can boast. As much as I tried to be cocky and magnetic, it never really worked.

I'm able to pen those songs you can hum along to, but the ones where you might go, "Wow, how did they do that?" are harder to tease out, and the domain of the truly-talented. What has changed as I get older, is that I dissect the arrangements of songs, instrument by instrument, to the point where the songs now sound quite different to me than they did in the past. In Another Script we were hamstrung by having only one guitar – I played 'rhythm' guitar on a few songs – so layering and intertwining wasn't something we could employ to colour the songs.

So that was that. End of band. Bon voyage.

I decided to go back to Tas too after a prolonged period of mental illness wouldn't budge. It took a few months but I recovered, and was raring to go, with something, anything.

13

Blackboard Jungle was a band made up of friends, as is always the case in Tasmania. (No-one *auditions*.) We had two well-blended guitarists, Martin and our friend Dave (from Lipstick.) Tim must have been otherwise engaged, so our mate Richard took over the drum seat. The *modus operandi* was to play something which merged country-punk, with swampy-punk, bluesy-punk, and old-songs-punked. After the Britishness of Another Script, this was an homage to American music, the more psychotically unhinged the better.

I'd become fixated with the American band The Gun Club and particularly their LP *Fire Of Love*. Jack White from White Stripes once said their song 'She's Like Heroin to Me' should be taught in schools. Not a good idea, but testimony to the song's brilliance. We played four tracks from the album. What I find strange about this, and what you probably need to be told about is that The Gun Club weren't the kind of group I'd normally like. They were brutal, ugly at times, loose-limbed, swinging like a loose railroad carriage. They sounded drunk and they sounded stoned, as raw as meat stripped off a live bull, and I liked it.

The singer of The Gun Club was Jeffrey Lee-Pierce, whose previous claim to fame had been presiding over the Blondie Fan Club. The band came together in LA which sounds all wrong. Weren't they vomited up by a satanic space monster in some filthy bog somewhere in the South? Lee-Pierce soon developed a reputation as a reasonably wretched personality. Members of the group would routinely leave 'for personal reasons'. In the documentary of his life, Lee-Pierce's death is looked upon with something like suppressed relief by his former cohort interviewees.

Another of the bands whose cupboard we raided was Jason and The Scorchers, a cowboy-hatted spur-booted, side-burned hard rock honky-tonk band from Texas. As well as updating songs by Hank Williams and Bob Dylan, The Scorchers had a swag of country-rock songs that suited us perfectly.

Somehow I'd temporarily turned away from pop (which was in a parlous state in any case) and begun drinking beer, in order to play 'drinking beer music'. I have a tape of a gig from Night Moves and our version of The Gun Club's 'She's Like Heroin To Me' is pounded out with extreme intent; tight, violent, threatening. Yes, I'd created another covers band, but at least this one had a kind of theme and physical aggression.

It was a good time for me and this was reflected in the devil-may-care attitude I had to Blackboard Jungle, and to life in general. When we first played in Hobart, it was the end of a week during which two friends I had met in Melbourne came down for a holiday. We traversed the East Coast, staying in a hotel my mother had arranged at a nominal fee through her work. The three of us ate pretty much every kind of edible aquatic creature on the menu, and then polished off several brandies before retiring to our room, drinking a slab, smoking joints, and watching The Young Ones. We continued on to Hobart the next day dodging log trucks, arrowing along the thin highway in a menacing parade.

By the day of the gig, by rights I should have been sleeping in our Hobart hotel, but I was young and indestructible. We played, to great acclaim and drank all that night. Jim Morrison's classic line, *"I woke up this morning and I got myself a beer"* was never truer.

The band were invited, along with a handful of Tasmania's best known groups to play at The Basin Concert, an annual event held at a gorgeous natural amphitheatre within walking distance of Launceston's CBD. With a pool, a cataract flowing into the titular basin, expansive lawns, bridges, a chairlift, walks and peacocks it's not surprisingly Northern Tasmania's chief tourist attraction. I can't recall who headlined the concert in 1986 although it's a good thing the weather co-operated because the stage was set up on top of the old bluestone change-rooms and had no roof.

Our performance was ... ok I guess, and hearing the backwash of our sound rebounding off the various walls of rock which cupped the basin was a kick. It was slightly surreal to know that my bass could be clearly heard by my mother at the family home three miles away. (Dad was at the gig – in fact he was in the 'wings' taking photos.)

Marshall was still our sound guy and recorded the gig, which perhaps wasn't such a good idea, because someone, I'm not sure who, was out of tune, and hence everybody was out of tune. It wasn't the kind of out of tune which would make you wince, but it's sullied my memories of the gig somehow.

For some reason – a combination of being an idiot and wanting to do something no other band would dream of doing, I suppose – I decided that, because I was about to get a new bass, I'd toss my old one off the stage during our last song. To pirouette and let it fly a la a hammer throw would have endangered the crowd, so I leant over the stage and slammed it bottom first onto the bitumen strip below.

Not only did the bass still work afterwards. It stayed in tune, all this with small rocks literally embedded in the bottom of the guitar's body. I gave it to a friend and he played it for years. He may well still be playing it. I think it was death-proof. Like something dreamt up by Stephen King.

14

Not long afterwards I was invited to join a band based in Hobart called The Fabulous Beagles. The story of this group and the groups which preceded it with several common members, is a tale of woe and heartbreak which makes my own copious 'nearly' moments pale in comparison. Welcome to the wild and wacky world of my friends Charles Touber, David Minchin. and Jarryl Wirth.

I tell this story at some length because something inside me feels like, 'there but for the grace of god went I'. And because it's either the quintessential cautionary tale or the greatest hard luck story in Australian Rock.

I was a bit too young to have become personally involved in this decades-long imbroglio but in 1975 a quartet of teenage hopefuls created a band called Beathoven. Naturally the template was to follow the path of the early Beatles but Beathoven honed this down to something specific and very canny. Having written some songs in the vein of the Bay City Rollers, and dressed up in a uniform of black boots, black suits with tails and top hats, the band began to play at schools during lunchtime.

They would very respectfully be approaching the heads of schools to ensure them that Beathoven played wholesome teen-friendly songs. Given the green light the band would then whip high school girls into a frenzy with their loud rock music and winning seductive smiles.

Their rise was meteoric. There's not really another word for it. By the time the group had saturated the school circuit with their irresistible cuteness, they were able to distill that following into bigger concerts at venues like the Hobart City Hall. The madness and hysteria of these gigs was identical to what was happening elsewhere in the world when teeny-bop bands played shows. A dangerous, delirious environment. Girls had made

Beathoven banners, homemade T Shirts, scarves. The eardrum-destroying squeal of girls screaming and wetting themselves was a renascence of the fabs in 1964.

Beathoven released two singles. 'Do You Remember The Time' was a limited pressing on the Hobart Candle label. The band then signed to EMI and the second 45 was 'Shy Girl'. Around this time Beathoven moved to Melbourne. Continuing the tactics of their time in Tasmania, schools were again on the band's radar. The effect was much the same. EMI though weren't happy with sales of the record and Beathoven received a 'Dear John' letter from EMI's boss, a man named John Kerr. The letter was dated 11th November 1975. Yes, really.

Rock impresario and generally repugnant dude Kim Fowley who had 'created' The Runaways, (concentrating less on the fact hat they could all play well, than how they looked, decking them out in corsets and hot pants) came to Australia as the guest of EMI on a talent quest. Hearing Beathoven and realising they were malleable, young and theoretically the next big thing, Fowley told his sponsor … EMI, yes EMI, that the band they had just jettisoned were the band he wanted to take under his glittery Machiavellian wing.

By now Beathoven were red-hot favourites to win the TV Week Best New Act. The gong instead went to Sports with the general feeling that Beathoven were too 'bubblegum' to effectively promote the rapid evolution of Australian music, and should therefore be overlooked.

The band were forced to change their name, which may have been wise anyway given its similarity to you know who (although it was pronounced Bayt-hoven.) The rebooted group was henceforth known as The Innocents. Fowley began writing songs for the band which was now curating and collecting material for an album.

But after Fowley left, the group wound to a financial and creative halt. Forced to do things like burn fence palings for warmth, the Innocents had left the world of pop stardom and been subsumed by a Dickens novel.

Enter RCA and some of their young gun session players. Charles had written an excellent song called 'Sooner or Later'. A world class pop song in fact, championed by stars like Elvis Costello and Nick Lowe. It was recorded, Monkees-style with gun guitarist Jarryl Wirth doing the parts usually handled by Charles and his Beathoven collaborator David Minchin. Bass parts were provided by Jim Manzie of naff retro outfit Ol'55. The band weren't entirely looked over, still taking on all the vocals. No-one at the studio could sing like original member Greg Cracknell. No-one in the *country* at that time could sing like Greg Cracknell. He could hit notes in places where angels fear to tread without switching to falsetto.

The band were duly booked on Countdown. Then RCA screwed the whole thing up by drip-feeding the record to radio stations and putting it in shops in different states at different times. What should have been a Top Ten hit Australia wide, and not just in Victoria, lingered in the midpoint of the charts in other domains before sinking. Since then 'Sooner Or Later' has become a staple in 'power pop' best-of lists worldwide.

'Sooner Or Later' went against the prevailing fashions of the time, which were vague and eclectic, but didn't embrace lean guitar pop unless it had the gimmickry, simplicity and noisiness of The Knack, or the sheer charismatic muscle of Cheap Trick.

Perhaps this is why the Innocents' follow-up 'Come Tonight', at least as good as its predecessor did nothing much. A punky, Undertones-y version of the song would be fascinating.

Fatigued by constant frustrations and Jim Manzie's priapic attitude to female audience members, as well as the palpable lack of success, the band essentially went into hibernation in the early '80s. Wirth and Manzie remained in Sydney. Touber and Minchin returned to Hobart, and in classic rock tradition had a major falling out. As a fillip to coincide with the millennium, a company called Zip based in Amsterdam released a compilation of all the Beathoven/Innocents material from the '70s and '80s.

In 1983 the two original songwriting members from the halcyon days of teen stardom, now estranged, formed their own bands, both of which played almost exactly the same thing. Charles created The Beagles, and David The Giant Hamsters.

The original line-up of The Beagles was Touber, Jim Manzie, who would fly-in from Sydney and play bass when needed, and Wirth, who I think may have been operating under a similar arrangement to fatten the guitar sound. The band would play a clutch of gigs to keep 'fans' interested, and then have a break to let the appetite build again.

When Manzie decided to move to LA to work on horror movie soundtracks, Charles needed to fill the vacancy. He'd heard the Another Script single, and was pleasantly surprised, and may have seen Blackboard Jungle. It was clear I could sing harmonies without too much tuition too. He gave me a call, and since Blackboard Jungle could easily work around Beagles gigs if we were given enough notice, I accepted the posting.

Playing in the Beagles was an experience in cognitive dissonance. From the times I'd chatted to him previously I was well aware that Charles was 'a bit of a smartarse'. What I didn't know though was that he viewed this musical project with boredom, laziness, cynicism and above all avarice. The seven deadly sins were almost covered. Once I had a grasp on the songs which were largely early Beatles numbers with bits and pieces of T Rex, The Monkees, Donovan and T Rex, and had briefly practised with Jarryl to consolidate our musical relationship, there were no more practices … *evaahh*. The song list remained the same for a year, then we added one song.

Charles was a charming front man and I think he enjoyed gigs, sometimes, but often enough *all* of us seemed to be going through the motions, stimulated only by the knowledge that we were making very, very good money. I mean, eight hundred to nine hundred dollars per night. Each.

The feud between Charles and David was precipitated, I think, by disputed songwriting credits, naming rights, and probably royalties. This didn't stop David joining The Beagles onstage one night. Immediately it was clear that he and Charles had a special relationship. My presence was barely acknowledged and the two of them were exchanging the kind of "We have a secret world and you're not in it" glances you sometimes see when you watch Lennon and McCartney.

The band was actually very tight and I enjoyed playing with Jarryl who was the best guitarist I'd worked with, and was also something of a Melbourne legend, having been a member of one of the very first punk bands in the country, The News.

On New Year's Eve Blackboard Jungle supported The Beagles which was more a convenience thing than a match of like-minds, or like-music. It was a busy night for me, and an enjoyable one. In Hobart the Beagles could fill a six hundred head capacity venue without trouble. It wasn't up to me anymore to fret about whether anyone would turn up.

I'd usually stay at a largely decrepit house in Sandy Bay shared by Charles, his girlfriend Polly and their friend Chris. There was no door on the toilet so you had to hold a large poster against 'the gap' for privacy. The rugs and carpets were threadbare and the oven was a museum piece. Still, the views were good.

The Innocents was not an entirely dead-in-the-water enterprise. Charles and Jarryl, along with sometime member and friend Rob Smith who could play almost any instrument, recorded a pro-demo of a song called 'Wrong Galaxy' and made a film clip, mostly consisting of footage from the Rest Hotel in Milson's point which was our home base for gigs. The song was played on Rock Arena, but the band had no record deal, no label interest, and no other songs, so all anyone could do was admire the track … and then forget about it.

As summer came to a close, I knew that once again I would have to split. If I chose Melbourne there'd be no band. The Beagles however had gigs booked in Sydney, and Marshall our sound guy had just moved there – he'd bought a recording studio, at the age of twenty-one – and there was a spare room at his new place. That was good enough for me. I had been a peripatetic sort of character, so trying out a new city seemed logical. The gigs would be a good financial foundation, rather than anything to really look forward to. I'm glad I was realistic about this because Beagles gigs were almost immediately irritating, even more mercenary than those in Tasmania.

Also irritating was Marshall's girlfriend – I should say that we get on well now – who for some reason rubbed me up the wrong way, so I jumped at the chance to live instead with 3 young women in Newtown in a large two-level terrace house. They were friends of Charles and also fans of the band, but from an insider and somewhat cynical position, so Linda and Tess in particular would be especially harsh if we weren't up to par. Up to par was a kind of mountainous peak the Beagles struggled with in Sydney mostly because we had no permanent drummer and often had to hire guys on the day. Some were sensible enough to keep it simple on the songs they were unsure of, and interact more fully on the songs they knew. Then there was Larry. Larry didn't seem equipped to count past three on his watch let alone behind a drum kit. It was the most aggravating and unprofessional musical experience of my life, but Charles insisted that we press on all night.

The Beagles, as far as I know, didn't play after the middle of 1987. Meanwhile on the flipside of that coin, The Innocents were dormant but hadn't quit. A Beathoven compilation LP, *No Hit Wonders From Downunder*, was released by Glenn A Baker, impresario and annoying music talking head. (He'd be called on by the media to comment whenever someone died.) The songs were pleasant enough, if naïve. Kim Fowley may well have sniffed out some royalties. Baker's assessment that the Innocents were "Perhaps the greatest Power Pop band in the whole world since the demise of the Raspberries" was a little hyperbolic, but then Raspberries were a genius band who also suffered a death by a thousand cuts in the fickle US scene of the '70s.

A few years later, the Amsterdam label Zip took the LP, rebranded as *Here We Come*, and added a second CD of Innocents demos – stronger material recorded sometimes alone by the various band members. In Europe interest in the band simmered along in Power Pop circles, and some of the group's songs were placed in movies.

Other albums followed in the noughties; *'Pop Factory'* – all new material. And then *'Teardrop Kiss'*. Both LPs were excellent. Charles and Rob Smith were now the core of the band. In fact, they were the sole songwriters. Greg Cracknell's wonderful voice was still utilised. Jarryl had drifted away.

The band, with David Minchin now back on guitar and vocals – I know it's confusing – played in London, Tokyo, and Hamburg in 2007, and were feted by ex-Beatle stylist and friend Astrid Kirccher. They took a request from Cynthia Lennon, and recorded a song with Tony Sheridan who had done the same with the Beatles as his backing band in 1960. Now in the overall scheme of things, these are not great earth-shaking moments in rock, but they do demonstrate that The Innocents weren't just another bunch of be-wigged chancers hoping to entertain tourists looking for a note-perfect fix of 'Please Please Me'.

(*Teardrop Kiss*, as with so much of The Innocents output, was badly promoted, badly distributed, released by a surprisingly inept label and received no airplay in Australia. If someone had paid *me*, I would have put my publicist's hat on and made certain at least that the record didn't sit in a warehouse gathering dust.)

I'm not sure The Innocents will ever officially split up. The one record per decade thing is probably unhelpful in trying to build another run at the retro-world where denizens meet as though part of a secret cult. I would have liked to have been more a part of The Innocents journey, but to be truthful, there's no talent I could have offered that wasn't already well catered for. Perhaps a song here and there, but Charles may not have allowed me that luxury. Watch 'Sooner or Later' and 'Come Tonight' on You Tube. They really are something.

The best thing about my time in Sydney was the house I shared which backed onto the Sandringham Hotel where bands played every night, with 'matinees' on the weekend. Our household would always go to see Secret Seven on Monday nights and the place would be choc-a-block. Secret Seven were not wholly unlike The Beagles but their tunes were more diverse and a little more obscure, with many one hit wonders from the '60s getting another run, along with bubblegum favourites like 'Build Me Up Buttercup'.

Sydney was tolerable but I missed Melbourne and my new job, which was similar to several that came before it, working in stationery, was a pain. I never left the office and had a heavy workload of invoicing and filing to complete every day. For the first time there was an element of dread to getting up. The business was also on the North Shore so I had to take two trains, then walk some distance to get there.

I did join Sydney Uni Soccer Club and was playing at a pretty high level (perhaps because I'd avoided having any egregiously bad games.) In any case, life in Sydney collapsed when I succumbed to mental health problems again. I did my best to shake free with the help of a doctor, but psychologically, being ill and so far from home convinced me I wouldn't get well unless I returned to Launceston to recuperate. So when The Beagles decided they'd fleeced Sydney, and would return to their various home bases, and with me not exactly feeling tickety-boo I left Sydney too. I was back to square one.

15

I was pottering about in Launceston doing nothing very much when I fell in love with a posh bisexual art-terrorist called Maura, who essentially set me up, took me to the park and seduced me at the swings. Maura was engaged to a merchant banker and was about to move to the UK. The timing wasn't great. The whole thing was doomed, and terribly painful, and weighed heavily on me for a long while, but it did give me some material for songs.

Most of my tunes are about someone or other, even if vaguely or obtusely. I don't really want to make a list of songs here and tell you who they're *about*, because it would mean nothing to you, and might horrify the people who had never suspected the connection. A friend in Perth did ask me once if a particular song was about her. I lied and said it wasn't. You tend to exaggerate heartache in a song. I don't think all those country songs are bastions of verisimilitude. That kind of lachrymose tragedy is inflated for effect.

Having already thrilled to the epochal debut Jesus and Mary Chain album, *Psychocandy* – a minimalist assault of uncontrolled feedback, two note solos – often slightly out of tune – and Spector-esque melodies delivered in a lazy echo chamber drawl – I was even more astounded by the sophomore release *Darklands* in 1987. With a cleaner feedback-free production, drum machines and a more haunting sound, I could scarcely believe how good it was. Gorgeous direct pop music. The single 'April Skies' became something of a standard for the groups I played in, because it was simple and hypnotic. I was inspired. I thought, 'I can do this.' I would react like this often when I saw bands in Melbourne. I'd go home and want to write songs. This didn't happen with movies for example. I had no idea how to go about making a movie. Especially … let's say *Aliens*. You can't make a sequel to *Aliens* in your bedroom. (Actually, there are SF nerds who probably can.) But you can make a rough recording of a Power Pop classic

The JAMC's follow up, *Automatic* was pretty good but after that they didn't seem to know what to do. They'd used up their repository of four or five chords, and rode a musical merry-go round into the '90s. The JAMC had changed the face of music then effectively left the building. You could argue that the entire shoegaze movement spearheaded by my Bloody Valentine and Slowdive owed its very existence to the Mary Chain. They burned hot and flared out, soon rewriting the same few songs, but leaving behind a vital legacy. With all the songs in the world to choose from The Pixies covered the JAMC's 'Head On' in a tribute of no little significance.

Across the Atlantic Sonic Youth were the alternative *group-du-jour*. I purchased their third album *Sister* on the strength of the reviews. It was a brutal record built on crazy guitar tunings and coruscating riffs. It still surprises that these discs were available at my local record store, because the teenage girls behind the counter were more used to selling large quantities of the *Dirty Dancing* soundtrack. Try dirty dancing to Sonic Youth and you'd be nursing a herniated disc. The group's masterpiece was Sister's follow-up *Daydream Nation*. Most people probably remember where they were when they first heard the opening tracks, 'Teenage Riot' and 'Silver Rocket'. The group made consistently great records for the next decade at least. Completely unique and in a class of their own.

With my pretty shoddy history of not taking much interest or not being attracted to a lot of black music – I should say I did own a lot of Chuck Berry, Little Richard etc., and at least one Marvin Gaye record; still not that great a mitigation – I was finally seduced by the sheer funky enjoyment of the early rap heavyweights. I was late to the party of course, but acquired *Raisin' Hell* by RUN DMC. And not just because Aerosmith were on it. That was rap's first example of cross-breeding (on 'Walk This Way'), but 'It's Tricky' was my favourite track. I'd never heard a kick drum that made my woofers work double time just to not disintegrate.

Culturally RUN DMC became, without setting out to do any more than be true to themselves, the most important rap artists of the '80s. (The political soothsayers were Grandmaster Flash, followed by Public Enemy. I owned the first two PE albums in the late 80s, but they were sometimes so intensely polemical and physical, I'd feel like a punching bag and need a break.)

I took recourse in the antic behaviour and rap-metal of Beastie Boys, who were shouty, immature, sexist – they later apologised for some pretty ugly stuff – and a chaotic rap version of the Sex Pistols. (They began as a regular punk band after all, before appropriating rap, not cynically, but naturally.) Their whiny voices on *License To Ill* and earth-shaking drums and guitars – 'Fight For Your Right (to Party)' was, crudely, the same riff as Deep Purple's 'Smoke On The Water' – were irresistible. They reminded me of the funny smartarses I went to high school with, except with beats. Beastie Boys not only became phenomenally successful very rapidly, straight outta Brooklyn and up to Number One, they subsequently joined the club of the many bands whose second LP was ten times better than the first and sold (literally) a tenth as many copies.

Paul's Boutique the follow up to *License To Ill* is a rap-funk masterpiece. Pieced together as a sonic jigsaw of samples and rhymes it's the kind of record which reveals new delights every time you listen to it. Endlessly. I had a conversation with a friend of mine recently and we decided, given the entire oeuvre of Beastie Boys, that they may have been the best and most influential band since the end of the '60s. For two decades they had a stranglehold on the album charts and popularity in all domains even when Eminem, Jay-Z, Snoop Dogg, Li'l Wayne, Notorious B.I.G and others threatened to unseat them. In 2019 Beastie Boys remained one of the Top Five selling rap acts in the US, more than thirty years after forming. (MCA a.k.a. Adam Yauch died in 2014 and the band quit.)

It might seem out of kilter considering the rest of the bands I'm talking about to spend time on the music of Beastie Boys, but something about the group remains important in my life even though I admit they never influenced my own musical choices or songwriting. That would be taking cultural appropriation to ridiculous levels. I've been to more Beastie Boys shows than any other band and have never been anything but astonished, especially when the group would don guitars and drums and 'play' live. The bass intro to 'Sabotage' should be an audio display at the Smithsonian.

16

I would deflect myself from the worries of a pretty bad year (the year being 1987) by taking over a spare room at home and recording a bunch of so-so songs on four-track. My reliance on a variety of effects to camouflage my clumsy playing meant everything sounded a bit like The Mary Chain. I'd experimented now and then with some stuff that was in the same vein as The Beatles' 'Revolution No.9'. Song-scapes consisting entirely of samples and noise. These were probably better than my efforts at writing actual songs. I remember my brother saying that when he'd heard some of these speculative arty pieces that he'd been "completely freaked out." They did, in a small way, allow me to vent about my ongoing struggles with depression. Conventional music doesn't really carry much clout in conveying extreme distress and disconnection from the real world. Reverb played through echo through sustain through a drum machine through a guitar through a vocal is more effective, all of it slowed down by fifty beats a minute does the trick. The horror … the horror …

Once I'd again recovered, I was mostly concerned with enjoying an uncomplicated life which would be punctuated by getting up, strapping on the bass, and stealing songs. I had one eye on returning to Melbourne so the new group, The Outstanding Amount had a built-in obsolescence which ensured it would all be pretty casual. Strangely the band still strikes me as being perhaps the most authentic and enjoyable of all my groups, because the song-list although leapfrogging through styles just as much was somehow cohesive, the songs complemented each other and the sound was consistently raw and intimate.

My then friend Mark who I'd met when I returned from Sydney and who had played bass now and then for Blackboard

Jungle and on some of my recordings, had a background in gospel, folk, minimalist pop and a style he'd christened "thrashabilly." He played a semi-acoustic electric guitar and a semi-electric acoustic guitar. It was the kind of band where egregious mistakes were encouraged.

(Mark was an actively proselytising Christian who had punctuated his busking days in the Launceston Mall with a bunch of Mumbo Jumbo preaching about God. From the moment he told me he used to speak in tongues I was fearful he'd do it again, in my presence, and I'd have to go and read a book or hide behind the couch or something until he was finished. We tried to keep religion out of rock'n'roll. Moreso me than him I suspect. It wasn't a topic I wanted to broach or an argument I wanted to have. His inflexible conservatism and starchiness, until he put a guitar on and went doo-lally, made it hard to warm to him completely, and he tucked his shirts in, but I suppose we initially compromised enough to get by. He had already formed the Fish John West Reject and the other members at that time were fairly committed Christians too, including Tim from Another Script, so as an atheist it wasn't something I wanted any part of.)

The Outstanding Amount's song-list was mouth-watering for fans of no-frills pop, rock and country. There were a few Violent Femmes tunes, some Modern lovers, Velvet Underground and Go-Betweens songs, a copy of the Triffids' version of 'You Don't Miss Your Water' (covered widely by soul acts and white guys with slick hair in black suits), a song which had the effect of bringing at least two audience members to tears every time we played it. We did some of the more organic Dylanesque Beatle singles like 'You've Got To Hide Your Love Away' and 'Baby's In Black' a few of Mark's appropriated yokel anthems like 'Muleskinner Blue's performed by too many country artists to list here. The idea was to keep the instrumentation raw and the vocals sweet.

The Velvet Underground somehow infiltrated everything we played. Even in 1991 I was ripping off bands that had ripped off the VU (The Wedding Present, The Wonderstuff) on at least two songs I wrote on the second Fish John West Reject album – yes, I joined the band, and yes, we'll get to that.

None of the groups I've played in have had any tangible connection to the Velvets; not the location nor the hatching from a multi-media conglomerate called The Plastic Exploding Inevitable, not the part-creation of the group in an artist's loft called The Factory by a famous post-modern Polish white-haired baked-bean obsessed svengali and print-maker, nor the heroin issues, nor the German female singer (in the early years.) The fact that the Velvets were largely informed by life in New York, and knew what and where the subway was didn't bother us. We lived with our parents and didn't swallow anything stronger than paracetamol – very responsibly. Somehow, we still tapped into the Velvets vibe.

As the years went on the VU's progression from art-project to more conventional rock band was tangible. It was still clear however that however they spun it, nobody would ever buy a Velvet Underground record when the Velvet Underground were still together. Eventually Lou Reed went solo and became the leather-clad scourge of interviewers everywhere.

(I had my own femme fatale at the time, with whom I was quite infatuated, and who was at all times wholly unpredictable. When we arranged to meet, she wouldn't show. When I was at the flat where I would hang out at with my friend Sue, watching TV, or designing band posters, she'd turn up unannounced. Something about this tantalising situation gave that November a piquancy that the relaxed nature of the band merely enhanced.)

This sunny time especially suited the upbeat mood of our Jonathan Richman and the Modern lovers covers. Richman began his journey as a Velvets obsessive, and recorded a self-titled (*Modern Lovers*) LP in 1973 which featured 'Roadrunner' (along with 'Wild Thing', almost certainly the most straightforward rock song in history.) So unadorned by chords is the song that the Sex Pistols managed to do a reasonable cover of it before any of them could really play. The rest of that record was shamelessly derivative of the Velvet Underground, excepting the vulnerability of the lyrics which veered from obtuse and hilarious (*'No one ever called Pablo Picasso an asshole'*) to a little disturbing on 'Hospital' and achingly maudlin on 'Girlfriend'. "*g-i-r-l-f-r-e-frend.*"

In the transpiring years Richman, sometimes in tandem with various versions of the Modern Lovers, stripped the sound back even further and now and then to nothing but the audience clapping, which is as meta as it gets, as he sang about the (literal) minutiae of life ('Hey There Little Insect') and penned lyrics such as *'Dee doidy doidy doidy do de doik doik dittle.'* (to rhyme with 'little'.) If it wasn't for tunes like 'I Was Dancing In The Lesbian Bar' you could buy a six year old a Richman record as a perfect introduction to pop. The Bostonian man-child did cover 'The Wheels Of The Bus' after all, although even a six year-old might find that a tad *declasse*.

The two note lead breaks were mostly cribbed from early Elvis and Bill Haley, and the rhythms from Bo Diddley. Richman had gone maximum geek in the '70s and never bothered with any reinvention for the next thirty years. He was an eccentric but very savvy guy who you imagine must have known just how seductive his deceptively elemental rock'n'roll nursery rhymes would be, and honed that simple joyfulness into pure art and a unique place in pop history.

Playing crowd-pleasing Richman tunes like 'The Beach' and 'Chewing Gum Wrapper' (about a chewing gum wrapper … it's not a metaphor) enabled The Outstanding Amount to become very, very popular. We mostly played in a small bar in Launceston – a kind of snug. The door would be closed and the house full sign would go up before we began to play. The gigs were profitable and sometimes the girl I mentioned, Melita, would show up too. I don't think I've enjoyed playing music at any time as much as I did that spring in The Outstanding Amount.

On a Friday evening in early 1988 at Night Moves, The Outstanding Amount played their last show in a five band bill which included a re-convened Blackboard Jungle, who had gigged sporadically throughout 1987 with an unsatisfactory changed line-up and an unsatisfactory song-list. There were three bands on between the two I was part of so I went home and changed my hair and clothes. My cunning identity disguises confused even people who knew me, who thought I might have been replaced by an imposter as per Paul McCartney.

Blackboard Jungle though wanted to go out on our own terms in as big a way as would be possible in a small provincial city with an even smaller alternative scene. The manager/band booker Grant wanted to help but had slightly cold feet as far as allowing us a headline slot on a Saturday night when Night Moves was still a 'club' for stenographers, accountants and builders who were there to get pissed and dance to INXS songs. Our dedicated fanbase couldn't really compete with this much-needed critical mass of … I hesitate to say bogans again. But there, I said it.

This was going to be well and truly it for the band. Dave was off to Queensland. I was making preliminary plans to return to Melbourne, and our drummer Potsy was getting married and moving to Hobart.

I was, I suppose you could say, in a weird mood. Weird progressed to ropeable when I was told that we had to play before a ghastly slick covers band called Dinner Time. This I should say, and in retrospect, was not THAT BIG A DEAL. I can see that Grant (or Beauy as he was known) was stuck between a rock and a hard place. He wanted to thank us without shooting himself in the financial foot. There was even talk (mainly from me) that we shouldn't play. Uppity rock star stuff. Anyway, we played, signing of with the Stones' 'No Expectations'. Mark took over on bass for the song and I spent most of it lying on my back making rude hand gestures to the crowd.

Having done our thing, we retired to the small band room, where I proceeded to kick the shit out of the door. It wasn't the sturdiest piece of lumber and split in half fairly easily, especially under a pretty crazed assault. The lower portion was hanging off by a hinge when Dave delivered the coup de grace and sent the whole thing flying into a corridor.

It didn't seem sensible to hang around, so I packed up my guitar and hoofed it out the emergency exit. This set off an alarm and a bouncer came to investigate. Surveying the scene of destruction and spotting my brother looking somehow sheepish and at the very least an accessory, he punched Martin in the head.

There was a party later on and it was only there that I was told what had happened. Martin was uninjured and unfazed and, after all, Blackboard Jungle had indeed gone out in a blaze of rock'n'roll glory.

17

I was having a good time and keeping busy, but rather than that spurring me to stay put and keep doing what I was doing, Melbourne beckoned again. Mark (from the Outstanding Amount) had returned to his more serious project, the aforementioned Fish John West Reject and the group re-established themselves in Melbourne too. The brief lifespan of the Outstanding Amount was done.

As much as playing had always been enjoyable and I'd reached a standard where I was able to pull the moves *and* mostly hit the right notes, it was music journalism that I wanted to pursue. I was better at that, I thought, than singing or bass-playing or penning songs, even though my experience was limited. As a kid, and an avid reader of rock papers, I could more readily see myself in a room full of hairy ne'er-do-wells clattering away on typewriters and arguing with lipstick-and-kohl feminists through a smoky fug, than hanging out in a backstage bunker drinking champagne with 'band-aids'.

These ambitions were largely sidelined by the other options available to me at various times in the '80s. Which is to say the bases seemed to be covered by staff writers at the papers. I had had one article published in RAM at the end of 1984 – a review of the year in Tasmania, which was included with a group of pieces about SA, WA etc. It was a lucky strike in the sense that the editor may have been thinking "If only we had something about Tasmania," on the day that something about Tasmania did, in fact, arrive. I had to use a pseudonym in order to talk about Another Script and to say unkind things about bad bands which featured people I knew. I was pleased of course, and surprised that I was also paid, but the days of apoplectic excitement about being published were over.

When I lived in Sydney, I wrote a pretty sloppy piece for RAM about Secret Seven (which didn't get a run) when that band released a single and I also applied for work as a copywriter at either JJ or JJJ (for which I was thanked for my interest.) I didn't feel that I had a foot in any door, and eventually presumed that the office job, and ongoing Beagles gigs would be my unsatisfactory lot in life. I really didn't have the confidence to be bullish about gatecrashing any area of the media, even though that approach may well have worked.

When I arrived back in Melbourne in early eighty-eight I set about getting published with more determination because otherwise I might have ended up flogging stationery again.

I received a lucky break when an expat Tasmanian who worked at The Melbourne Times, a free inner-city home-delivered paper (which was light on editorial but big on real estate advertising) invited me to review some records. The first of these was, *The Story Of The Clash* a double LP (when vinyl was still the most common, or at least beloved format) and to be honest it wasn't a great piece of writing, but I knew the subject. This was followed by a review of The Hollowmen, a local band fronted by Coodabeen Champion and hero of Paul Kelly, Billy Baxter. I decided that since I was now a rock critic, I should criticise, which I did in a mild but probably snooty way.

It seemed to me that a CV was never going to get me anywhere, and that as a musical and literary auto-didact I should just write-send-repeat until I either went mad or became a default journalist.

RAM was teetering, although it struggled on for another year, but was in any case based in Sydney, which was fine when I was a reader, but a harder obstacle to navigate as a contributor/writer who wasn't able to 'drop in', say hello and smoke dope.

Another nationally distributed magazine was the Melbourne-based weekly Juke which hadn't spawned the explosion of journo-as-rock-star pre-millenial 'influencers' for which RAM was known (not unlike Richard Neville's OZ), but did have the advantage of being owned by David Syme, publishers of the Age who had fairly deep pockets so there were none of the concerns that a few badly performing issues would mean the end of the party.

A few other advantages enjoyed by Juke were an up-to-date national gig-guide, a variety of charts-by-genre, and an up-to-date news page. Juke would go to press as late as possible and be delivered efficiently all over the country. It boasted a full colour glossy cover too while Ram had retreated into a cost-cutting bi-colour design. So, Juke had the edge in a few ways and also stayed on the straight and narrow by sticking to big guns as its cover stars whereas RAM was always the moral winner in the how-do-you-sleep-at-night stakes) took its chances with independent acts they believed in, much in the vein of NME and the nascent capital city street press.

Juke's picaresque editor, Christie, a kind of loveable rogue with perhaps too much rogue, would sometimes source (without attribution) articles from overseas magazines, some via prior arrangement, and some without permission at all. Hence some readers would think that, for example, the legendary Nick Kent at the NME was based in Melbourne.

None of this was enough of course to put me off from believing Juke might be a good fit for my talents, such as they were.

My first speculative crack at being published was with a live review of a band called Crashland. They were a three-piece led by Ash Wednesday, a punk luminary and part of Melbourne's music 'mafia'. He played a keyboard loaded with samples, mostly crushing power chords. The vocalist was a demonic dervish called Lyn Gordon, part Chrissy Amphlett part Iggy Pop. I liked them a lot and felt that, even if my thoughts on them remained unread, that it was worth giving it a go. I was smart enough to keep the review down to about three-hundred words, which would make it the third of the three live reviews usually published on the same page each week.

I would have included a polite 'For Your Consideration' letter and sat back, hoping for the best. A few Mondays later, there it was, there I was, accompanied, pleasingly, by a photo (of the band, not me.) This was a good start but no guarantee that it was anything more than a flash in the pan. I waited a few days then phoned Christie and introduced myself and he told me that Ash Wednesday had phoned to tell him he'd loved the review, so I asked him if he was interested in a review of the Cheap Trick show I'd just been to. Christie said yes, and the rest is unreliable history. Juke should have had a reviewer at the gig anyway, but that's how slightly sloppy the paper was.

(Cheap Trick were fine of course but had just released a pretty bad 'comeback' album, from which had come a pretty bad chart-topping single, 'The Flame'. There was a touch of pushback now in my attitude to them and their centrality in my life had long faded. I wouldn't have missed it mind you, and saw them on both the nights they played in April 1988 and twice that November when they surprisingly returned.)

With my lengthy Cheap Trick piece published I took the next step and visited the Juke offices in town to introduce myself. Christie was not what I'd imagined, because I hadn't imagined a short, cheerful Sri Lankan in platform shoes. The deputy editor, Byron, was about my age with a model's visage and long brown hair. (I wondered about which side of the political or ethnic divide Christie was positioned on, but that was made clear when Byron asked Christie if he wanted a "Tamil burger" for lunch.) I was invited to raid the cupboards for new release albums and took full advantage. I think a few things were immediately clear to the Juke people; I was responsible and far from starry-eyed, I wrote with sufficient knowledge and authority, was clearly enthusiastic, and would deliver what they wanted without delay. My first clutch of LP reviews were all given a run, and I was well and truly in.

The one thing I had no experience of and something I had to learn by trial and error was how to interview a rock star. The first few acts I spoke to, and who spoke into my Walkman (ah … sweet memories) were local hopefuls and my natural curiosity served me well. It just wasn't difficult as long as you'd written down what you wanted to ask. The boring bit was transcribing what was on the tapes, sentence by sentence.

So that meant doing the interview, transcribing the interview, writing the piece with a pen onto something we old people called paper, and then using my manual typewriter to knock up something close to a final draft.

For interviews with acts from overseas I would be able to attach a microphone with a suction cup to my phone and plug the other end into the Walkman. Phoners, as they were known, were never entirely satisfactory. They didn't convey body language, facial expressions, and other subtleties of communication. And they generally only lasted twenty minutes.

My first phoner, and an incident I still feel embarrassed about, was my chat with Steve Cropper. Steve Cropper, voted in several magazines as one of the greatest guitarists of all time. Steve Cropper, the long-haired guy from The Blues Brothers. Steve (fucking) Cropper. I think I still have the tape somewhere. I must have recorded some demos over the top. Now the interview itself was fine. Fine in the sense that I knew barely anything about Steve Cropper but still managed to ask him questions. I'd heard 'Green Onions' by Booker T & The MGs, on which he plays guitar. I'd seen the Blues Brothers. I may have had a record company bio. But I was blithely unaware that … deep breath … he was a member of the Stax house band and had co-written and produced a bunch of Otis Redding records including 'Sitting On The Dock Of The Bay.' That he co-wrote 'Knock On Wood'. That The Beatles wanted to work with him. That Keith Richards had described him as "perfect man," etc. etc.

The problem was, because I had a few things to do, I just didn't get round to the Steve Cropper article. It remained unwritten, and Christie, with enough on his mind, never asked for it. So, one of the legendary figures of '60s soul had wasted twenty minutes of his life on me, an inept music hack from some hick town in Australia.

18

The great thing about being a journalist is that you can ask questions of people that you would never normally get to ask. If you meet a rock star under some sort of social circumstance, you can't bombard them with peculiarly personal questions like "What kind of childhood did you have?" This would appear, in that context, to be a really weird thing to ask, but as a journalist you have something close to *carte blanche*. You're able to be mildly confrontational or at least cheeky ("Why do you think that record didn't sell?") and you don't have to show deference. As a fan who meets a star, you're automatically saying "I look up to you! I wish I was you! Or at least your friend!" As a fan *and* an interviewer you get to have a fairly even-handed chat and you know you won't freeze or gush or generally fall prey to acting like a lickspittle.

This dynamic was highlighted a while back when I began dating the mother of a quite famous Australian actress and pop star. Now and then there would be Skype or Zoom hook-ups during which I'd be called on to participate, so I'd sheepishly say hello and then retreat fast. Had I been writing about said star, I'd have had plenty to say. For example, "Did you feel you were under pressure as a well-known public figure to transition successfully from acting to music?" which would have been a conversation-killer if she'd just pinged her Mum and sister for a chat.

The one time when I was forced to ask a question I was uncomfortable with was when, for some reason, I was commissioned to interview someone (possibly Rebecca Gibney) for TV Week. It was requested of me that I should ask the 'talent' if they were "seeing anyone." This was an excruciating moment and Rebecca (?) deflected the query politely and, having sensed my squeamishness, not without sympathy.

But when you interview someone they are obliged to tell you *something* when they might not want to tell you *anything*, Because this is their career, not exactly on the line, but certainly not needing to be damaged, unless they want to develop a terrible reputation. This was the case when I did a phoner with Kurt Cobain. (There is no way here I can avoid namedropping. It goes with the territory I used to roam.) it was a strange time for Nirvana. *Nevermind* was selling in insane amounts and this punk-grunge band were now global behemoths. Anyway, Kurt had had a pretty long and rough night and someone had decided it was a good time for him to get a phone call. First thing in the morning. Bad move. Even then … even THEN, in the maelstrom of success and the pressure of sudden fame, the guy was polite enough to kinda have a go. I asked him if there was a temptation, now that *Nevermind* was making money for David Geffen hand over fist, to make the next record ridiculously extreme, maybe like Lou Reed's *Metal Machine Music*? And he said, "Well I dunno, we could always be more extreme by making a cheesy pop record." And that was a good answer. So let's imagine that Nirvana, rather than recording the abrasive, tetchy *In Utero, had* recorded a cheesy pop record, and that you heard it *here* in Juke, in my article first. Wow. See what I mean. These of course are known as 'scoops', and I can't say I've come close enough to one in order to shout "Hold the presses!"

I was in a bar with Lisa on the night that Pulp played in Melbourne and having freshened up, the band happened to wander into the same bar. Being the kind of bloke who never let's a chance go by, and more importantly, seeing that my quarry was at the bar by himself, I decided to say hello to Jarvis. I have to say he didn't *look* that happy, but anyway, I tried to initiate a conversation but he clearly wasn't really into it, so I just said "Oh well … enjoy the tour … bye" He was borderline rude, and disinterested at best. Fortunately, some of the other Pulp guys were happy to argue with me about Sheffield soccer teams. Some time later Jarvis was doing some sort of global radio hook up, and people were somehow able to phone in and ask a question. So that's what I did. Jarvis was a different person. Thoughtful, engaged. This is how the interview can often in no way reflect real life.

19

When Cheap Trick announced their second 1988 tour and the interviews were being dished out by their record company, Epic, it was axiomatic that I would be the one doing the interview for *Juke*. Before I'd even been asked which member of the band I'd like to talk to I said to Christie, 'I want to talk to Robin'.

It would not be the first time I had spoken to Robin. In 1979 Cheap Trick toured for the first time and played at Festival Hall in Melbourne. As soon as I got wind of the impending arrival of my heroes I bought a plane ticket, and I bought two concert tickets (for me and my friend Phil.) I don't remember much about the show. I was too hyped up to absorb much except the disbelief of being four rows away from the band. I guess this is what Beatles fans felt in 1964, except I wasn't screaming or peeing my pants.

After the concert we returned to our hotel and I set about phoning *other* hotels hoping to locate the band. It only took one call, to the Southern Cross, to get the good news. "They've changed their names," said the receptionist, when I quite stupidly asked if she could call them. "But they're in the bar."

Woooooooosh! … we hotfooted it up to Spring St and ran gasping into the hotel lobby. There seemed to be road crew relaxing and having a beer, but no band, then I turned around, and there was Robin. He of the golden hair, impossible cheekbones and pacific blue eyes. He held an outstretched hand and off we went, into a perfectly pleasant, grown-up conversation. Looking back, I think this chat said something about my future. Rather than gush or bumble, I just chatted. I got past the being overwhelmed bit and then went straight to curiosity.

Soon after, guitarist Rick Nielsen strolled out of the lift, and it was much the same. He was impressed that we'd flown over from Tasmania, and he actually knew a bit about the place.

Over the years I've met Rick and Robin again, after gigs; a few times backstage, and a few times in clubs. Robin has always been a lovely guy to talk to, but Rick can be prickly and Jarvisesque. The interesting thing is that I interviewed Rick (a phoner) in 1997, and he was fine. Was he in a better mood? Was it that he had an album and tour to promote?

It made me think that sometimes an interviewer who doesn't feel like asking questions, will be asking them of someone else who isn't that interested in answering them. But there is a pact between the pair. And the finished copy might be fabulous. Weird. Imagine the pressure which was on the Beatles to behave like Beatles in every city they visited, shanghaied at airports over and over again, and asked things like; "How do you find America?" ("Turn left at Greenland," Lennon quipped.) Eventually The Beatles stopped talking to anyone at all. That happened when there was no need. They couldn't get any bigger. They didn't need to promote themselves.

My phoner with Robin, almost a decade after the Festival Hall show, was fine. Unremarkable really. There was nothing too evasive about his answers even when I touched on the barren years when Cheap Trick sold about three copies each of a few dodgy albums. He managed to pronounce my name correctly, and that was the biggest surprise. I could have asked better questions, but that tends to be a corollary of the whole process. As soon as you hang up and think about how the whole thing went, there are always follow-up questions you realise have slipped past. The biggest challenge is to a) appear knowledgeable or do some serious research if necessary – this was never too easy before Wikipedia – and b) avoid the kind of clichéd Dorothy Dix questions a morning TV host might ask.

By the time the Cheap Trick interview was ready to go, I'd managed to secure a temporary staff position at Juke. Christie had gone on holiday, so Byron became editor, and I became deputy/features editor. I was now able to do whatever the hell

I liked, but what I wanted to do was to make Juke a better magazine. I made sure the Cheap Trick story was a double page spread, but they didn't make the cover. I'm not sure why that didn't happen. I took over the Barbed Wires news-gossip-tidbits column which prompted one longtime contributor to say, "What happened? Barbed Wires was actually funny this week."

Byron and I set up a film page and I got us on the list of media outlets to be invited to previews; champagne, nibbles, printed synopsis, a choice of photos, and a viewing in a cosy cinema without people slurping on Coke or eating popcorn. It also enabled me to interview a few directors which I just about managed to do without looking like a fool. I talked to a fellow called Dominique Derrudere about his film adaptation of The Charles Bukowski novel *The Most Beautiful Girl In Town* (rebooted as 'Crazy Love'.) Bukowski was American, the film was set in America, filmed in Belgium and spoken in French. I knew as much about the Belgium film industry as I did about quantity surveying, so I gently probed the director for some information about that, and then we talked about Bukowski and the tone of the film etc. etc. It was a case of hoping for the best and getting a reasonable result, but anything could have happened really. I didn't get round to chatting about how the film was utterly bleak. Very well-made but a tad nauseating. Then there was the necrophilia. And there am I asking how the weather is in Antwerp.

During my too-brief tenure, I made sure we didn't reprint anything from other papers, which was Christie's speciality, and most people seemed to think Juke improved noticeably when Byron and I had the reins. I was a judge for the Yamaha national band competition – more free food – and generally enjoyed the kind of perks you get when a load of major record companies are trying to be extra nice to you.

That working holiday didn't last sadly. Christie came back. The film page stayed, but the energy of Juke seemed to slide a little. It's not like Christie didn't work hard. Juke would have never got to the printers if he didn't. I just disagreed with some of his decisions.

For most of 1989 I wrote for Juke and didn't get up to much else. The Fish John West reject were becoming big, which didn't surprise me. I met plenty of new friends. My health was up and down, but I was freelancing again essentially, so there wasn't too much pressure. I had been in a brief relationship with a girl called Anna who sang in a local band and had the best voice I have ever heard. Like Harriet from the Sundays (who were around about at the same time) but with a bit more grit now and then. We met at a party and yada yada yada basically. She was funny and caustic, and still is I think. Anyway, it didn't quite work for me and being the sort of person who panics if that happens, I ended it.

Not long afterwards, her band released a single called 'Michael Told Me'. Now, there are three possibilities here; the name Michael, with its two even syllables may have just suited the rhythms of the music, or the Michael in the song was me ('*A brave heart always led / to someone else's bed*') or Michael wasn't me, but Anna did it to make me think it was me to take the piss. I still have no idea, and it was thirty years ago, so I can't *ask* her can I?

Speaking of women with amazing voices (rather than women who I dated) it was the year that Bjork emerged from the hypothermic chill of Iceland, with her band the Sugarcubes. At this point Bjork was enigmatic in the sense that I'd heard her remarkable performance on 'Birthday', but didn't know much else about her. Now we all know that she's bonkers, makes incredible music and videos, got in a few punch-ons at airports, didn't get on with Lars Von Trier, and is maybe not someone you'd imagine you could have a regular conversation with. I didn't know she was in a punk band called Spit and Snot. But there was no Wikipedia in 1989.

Bjork was delightful. I didn't know much about The Sugarcubes, or Iceland. At the end of our chat I knew just a little more about her band but plenty about Iceland. She invented an adjective, and I can still hear her say it. I asked if there was any light in Iceland in winter and she said, "It gets … twilighty." What a wonderful word. She also said, of the band's album, and the recording of it in New York that, "We had to go somewhere boring where there was nothing else to do." I don't think she was joking. It seems that when the sun comes out in Iceland, everyone goes batshit crazy and parties for six months.

The emergence of The Sugarcubes charming the world with their unique and spectral take on pop was an early signal point to what was to come in the '90s. Genre-merging and wild experiments. It wasn't John Cage and Miles Davis, but pop had at least broken away from its high-sheen complacency.

It was a time when female artists, or female fronted bands, were coming to the fore or hitting creative high points; Baby Animals, the Divinyls weren't too far away from their US hit 'I Touch Myself', Kate Bush released 'The Sensual World' and Madonna dropped 'Like A Prayer' ('dropped' wasn't part of music terminology back then by the way.) The Bangles lost their indie-rock cred but had a massive hit with 'Eternal Flame', Even Kim Wilde made waves with a great record, *'Close'* and did a promotional tour. I interviewed her at Warner Brothers and she was on her back on a couch, having hurt herself skiing in Japan. So I sat on a chair next to her, like a psychiatrist. The temptation to cross my legs, put a notepad on my knee and say "Tell me about your mother," was almost strong enough to go through with, but she might not have got the joke.

Wilde was struggling to regain her foothold in Australia after a flurry of hits in the early '80s. The strange things is that the album she was promoting, is excellent, and the single Never Trust A Stranger' was an absolute banger. If you want to listen to how pop sounded, how chart pop sounded, at the end of the

'80s that song has it all, sequenced bass, electro-beats, a massive pumping snare drum, synth-strings and a great tune. How it failed to chart when it was a top ten hit in the UK is a complete mystery to me.

We were a year away from the Riot Grrrl explosion, but at the other end of the spectrum there was the similarly feminist but less angry, very dressy-uppy and pop-tastic Voice Of The Beehive.

The band consisted of two American sisters, ex-child models, who had relocated to London (very wisely), seconded some locals including Woody from Madness and formed a band. I was a big fan of their wittily-titled debut LP *Let It Bee*, as were my friends. I was also a fan of Melissa and Tracy on a more … unrequited, never to be requited romantic level.

So the chance to speak with Melissa was something that made my sorry heart skip a beat. I couldn't have asked for more. I barely had to ask anything. I just gave her a bit of a push and off she went at a million miles an hour.

"Ow… I touched the kettle. Oh it's raining. I really don't mind the weather here, but I hate the trash. People leave it anywhere they like. Where was I?"

I'm not sure. You were just back in the US?

"Oh god, it was … so … fucking … boring … answering the same dumb questions fifteen times a day. And the food is CRAP. Anyway, we went clubbing and it was okay after that."

I didn't say what I was thinking – that a press junket to the US and a few days of interviews would mean, for me, that I was well and truly in the pop stratosphere. But I changed the subject.

"Do you watch Neighbours?"

"Yesssss, I do, and you sound like one of the cast!"

"Nooo."

"Well you have an Australian accent. You live in Melbourne, right? That's where they film Neighbours. Doesn't that drive you crazy?"

At this point I was pretty sure I was flirting with Melissa Brooke-Belland, in the sense that I probably wasn't, or she wasn't, with me, but maybe I thought I was, with her. We talked about Kylie ("She's breathtakingly beautiful and a fucking professional") About a scandal when she dissed model turned pop star Sam Fox ("You can talk about Reagan or Northern Ireland, or sexism. I just happened to be talking about CRAP.") and about the band, which is what I was supposed to be asking her about. It resulted in the kind of article that virtually 'writes itself' and those are always best.

Twelve months later I interviewed Voice Of The Beehive in the flesh. Having made no serious ground with their first LP, the band now had a hit on the boil with their hi-tech cover of the Partridge Family's 'I Think I Love You.' So, they'd flown out to do some TV. I was lucky to walk into the Hilton just as Melissa was arriving back from an outing. I introduced myself, and although she didn't know there was an interview, she was happy to guide me up to the rooms they were staying in. The whole band squashed into one room to answer a few questions, but mostly to just talk. Melissa (Missy) and her sis Tracy (Ray) both had a kind of aura about them. I'm not sure if Californians simply *look* different or whether pop stars look different. In any case, you wouldn't just walk past them without doing a double take.

"I've been to the fairy shop!" Missy said to Ray. "They tell you stories. So I said, 'Tell me a story about the moon.'"

Fun fact: Melissa now runs her own fairy shop business in Laguna Beach. So Melissa was in a good mood, and then Tracy's favourite ever play came on TV (Sam Shepherd's 'True West') and then the band's pre-recorded slot on *Hey Hey It's Saturday* came on, so there wasn't a lot of interviewing going on. Melissa was still able to have a quite amusing bitch about how she didn't like the production on their second LP. She just didn't seem to give a fuck about anything.

I'm going to go *off piste* a little now, but indulge me, please.

The most overlooked, or perhaps taken for granted, of all the female bands who emerged in the '80s were actually Bananarama. First there was the prolific nature and consistency of their hit-making. Ten Top 10 hits in the UK between 1983 and 1989, and another fourteen Top 40 entries. They've spent as many weeks in the charts as Queen, and Queen first charted in 1973 and still chart. Bananarama had Australian and US number one with 'Venus.' They were the consummate singles band, mainly because their albums didn't do that well. Their first single was a Swahili folk song, their second single in 1981 was 'T'Ain't What You Do (It's The Way That You Do It' with Fun Boy Three, written in 1939. This wasn't the normal way to launch your career. They co-wrote most of their subsequent hits until Stock Aitken and Waterman stepped in. This resulted in hits but SAW found the band far too much trouble to try to groom into a cookie cutter girl group.

This is not such a surprise since the band were so punk. What I mean by that is that they were art school drop outs who lived at the YWCA until Sex Pistol Paul Cook offered them a tatty room at his place. They began by singing backing vocals for people like Iggy Pop and The Jam. When female acts dressed in spandex, plastered in eye makeup, Bananarama wore overalls and sported bird's nest hair. It seemed that their whole career was a bit of a laugh that got out of hand, which is not to say they didn't work very hard to ensure they didn't end up back at the Y. None of the three had great voices but the blend was effective. They were unaffected, unpretentious, playful and the perfect band for schoolgirls (and boys) to mime along to in front of the bedroom mirror. Spectacularly ordinary, joyful and consistently enjoyable. It might seem like a strange choice, but if I'd been able to interview any band that I didn't it would have been Bananarama. Not Pink Floyd or Bob Dylan or Madonna or U2 … especially U2. I wanted a memory of Keren Woodward to give me the warm and fuzzies in later years.

What I missed out on as well as a chat with Bananarama was the longform interview where the writer spends time on tour with the band. Only magazines like Rolling Stone could afford these kinds of 'exclusives', where the artist would generally, at some point let their guard down a little, and the journalist would get more insight into the personality of their hosts. As well as flying all over the US as their guest. And staying in lush hotels. That was never going to happen.

20

In early 1990 I moved into a large apartment in Brunswick with Mark. I wallpapered the lounge with NME covers I'd cut from the magazines, which seems now to be an exhausting task and one which would leave behind a lot of blu-tak marks. Visitors were impressed however.

Half way though the year, Martin was asked to join the Fish when it was decided that the group's multi-instrumentalist and wizardly hippie Mark (another one) had become unreliable; missing practices, possibly a gig or two. Martin only played guitar so the sound immediately changed. His first show was at the Perth Entertainment Centre, supporting UB40. A baptism of fire. By the time he was about to head up the East Coast, the Fish were booted off the tour. It's not hard to see why. As much as UB40 had utterly sold out, from working class Brummies singing about unemployment, to expensively-suited crooners doing dull covers of songs like 'Red Red Wine', they did still have one foot in reggae, and several black members. The Fish, not with any malice, were playing a few profoundly redneck country-folk songs, hollerin' and a yelpin' through stuff which would have been originally released during the days of racial segregation. It wasn't a good fit, and I'm not sure who thought it was.

Only a few months after Martin was recruited, the band lost their bass player, Andrew, to family duties. He was a single Dad to two growing sons, so Mark asked if I wanted in. Without giving it much thought, other than succumbing to the lure of joining a band who had already laid the groundwork and done the 'struggling artists' bit, I said yes to the invitation.

With Martin and I in the band the sound was going to change – a lot. Gone was the harmonica, the banjo, the dopey songs which ex-Mark wrote. In came a loud electric guitar (although Martin was able to play mandolin and a few bits and pieces) and in came me, with some songs already written which Mark wanted to include in the set because he had a bit of a writer's block problem.

As well as the vintage stuff which I always dipped into, I was listening to The Wonderstuff, The Wedding Present, Pop Will Eat Itself – especially Pop Will Eat Itself. I was also fine-tuning a very Jesus and Mary Chain-influenced song. Essentially my own material had no similarity to the songs on the first Fish LP, or the band's live set from 1989, the energetic performances of which had led to their success.

Within a month of joining the Fish John West Reject, I had played sixteen gigs in four states. Trains, planes, vans and automobiles. I was still in my twenties and robust enough to have no qualms about the intensity of the touring. It was dull, uncomfortable, tiring, at times stressful, and I used to love getting home and collapsing into bed, but never did I think, "Oh I can't keep this up for much longer."

These tours did enable me to catch up with old friends and there were new romances and friendships which had a whiff of 'girl in every port' about them eventually. Forgive me. I was just a boy.

The drive to Sydney was patently the worst time you can have without poking out your eyeballs with knitting needles. We'd set off in the dark at about 7 am and be on the road for twelve hours or so, arriving in Sydney with enough time to spare to eat some KFC and set up before the show. Having played maybe 4 gigs we'd do the whole thing in reverse. One night when I was driving us home, I was pulled over in some dismal blot on the already tedious landscape by a typical country cop for going seventy km/h instead of sixty. He made us empty the van warning us that he'd better not discover any 'sharps'. None of us knew what a sharp was, and we didn't have a junkie on hand to explain. We'd often be drunk with exhaustion by the time we reached Albury/Wodonga, and that last stint was generally unsafe.

With the proceeds of tours and ongoing Juke writing I was comfortably able to pay rent, eat, and go out drinking. The issue with touring, especially with a lot of shows crammed together, and doubly especially if the guarantee isn't locked in, is that you need someone who understands money, and how much of it you should spend. Our manager Gary was very good at this. And a straight up guy. The fifth Fish if you like. Towards the end of the year when we became touring partners with Weddings Parties Anything, their manager, whose name I refuse to say, somehow convinced Gary that the fish needed … god knows what, an idiot (?) to look after gigs outside of Melbourne. Our normal practice of couch-surfing when on tour, was replaced by our being booked into of massive apartments in Milsons Point. This guy was spending our money hand over fist. Eventually Weddings gave him the heave-ho too, but for us, when we split, there was a bill for ten thousand dollars which this guy had clocked up, presumably under the impression we would soon be huge. I imagine he would have said something about 'the big picture'. The big wanker. Martin covered our debts, although I didn't realise he had. Martin wasn't the type to break this guys ankles. He should have asked me.

In early August we flew to Perth for two weeks of gigs and some recording at a studio called Planet, where plenty of bands had recorded plenty of great records. My ballad 'Sick Inside' was on the schedule. It was a very personal song to me, about a tough break-up, and I always sang it at concerts. On the day, Mark didn't think I was singing it well, and … I dunno … for some reason I deferred, and he sang it instead. It's pretty horrible, and I wince when I hear it. It said a lot about Mark who was a kind of accidental egoist. He didn't go out to fuck people over, but sometimes he did just because it was who he was. As a person he was too naïve to be calculating, but also too thin-skinned to accept criticism or understand irony if a joke was a gentle dig at him. I always felt like I was self-censoring in order to avoid hurting his feelings. Meanwhile he could trample all over other people's feelings without even knowing he was doing it. He probably thought he had to intervene on 'Sick Inside' but there was a sense of dismay amongst fans and friends when they heard the results.

Martin and Mark were thick as thieves which was fortunate. Martin could confide in Mark about things he wouldn't have felt uncomfortable divulging to me. This also took the pressure of me as far as being Mark's 'friend', which I was, but it was hard work. We all had other closer friends outside of the band anyway. My old diaries tell me I was *always* out at other gigs, or clubs, or visiting friends, or at parties.

I'd become accustomed to being the interviewee as well as interviewer, and there were plenty of media outlets in Perth especially wanting to get up to speed on Fish news. Somewhat paradoxically I suppose, I don't think I was ever much good as an interview subject. I'd drift off into discursive territory and probably came across as a bit cynical about the industry. I remember after a gig in Sydney, talking to Pete the bassist in Weddings and whining indulgently about the whole silly business of driving all over the place hoping crowds would show up. There was a pause before he said, "It's better than working in a bank."

It felt odd to be spoilt the way we were in the West in particular, because that attention seemed to put us 'above our station' if you like. When we arrived at the airport there was a big truck waiting, and several roadies who whisked our gear away in a trice. We did have one roadie at home in Melbourne, but hauling my own amplifier and speaker box around by myself, appeared to me to be an accurate indication of where we sat on the ladder of success and a method of keeping my feet on the ground. At the Shenton Park Hotel I arrived to find my bass rig set up, with my guitars tuned and sitting on stands. The microphones had been de-scummed with bursts of Glen 20, and my plectrums were taped to my mic stand. There was nothing for me to do.

The Fish were a pretty big noise in WA, and I suppose I didn't adjust to that level of 'fame' for want of a better word. Having said that, we weren't exactly the Rolling Stones. I was caught in a middle ground where the notion of 'successful' was a moot point. Yes, we were headlining Perth's major venue on a Saturday Night, much like The Angels did in Launceston all those years ago. But no, we weren't swanning in to town to play a sold-out Entertainment Centre. As much as we might have enjoyed this slightly elevated popularity, the time we spent in Perth was still very much budgeted down to the last petrol receipt.

The singles and album the Fish had already released, a few years earlier, hadn't burned up the charts in the West. We were still an independent band, and had none of the major label largesse which would have meant full page ads in various papers and maybe some TV. Even then the anticipation you could sense in the crowd at gigs was a buzz. The rise of the band had been extraordinary. It just concerned me a little that, all things considered, we may not have been that good.

At this point our setlist was a mixture of my new songs and the stuff the band played two years earlier, and ne'er the twain shall meet. It must have been confusing, and somewhere along this transitional path, the Fish lost some fans. Suffice to say we gained some others. And I imagine some, like swinging voters, weren't sure what to make of it all.

We recorded three songs in total in Perth then decamped to Whirled Studios in Richmond to finish the rest of what would be the second Fish LP. I'd written about half the album and the other songs were divided between Martin, Mark and Andrew (former bassist) as well as a cover of The Innocents' 'Sooner or Later' which the band had recorded some time earlier for a compilation CD of current acts covering Australian classics for 3RRR.

I'm not sure what was going on with Mark. He only wrote two genuinely new songs for the record, and one was an instrumental. Martin had written an excellent elegiac ballad which ended the record but Mark sang that one too. He also did the vocal on the opening track, 'Terrible News' which was one of mine, and I'm not sure how that happened either. Lennon didn't sing 'Yesterday' and McCartney didn't sing 'Come Together.' Mark kept nicking our songs.

Anyway, things got worse for any folky fans hoping for another LP like the first. I'd been listening to bands like Pop Will Eat Itself and Jesus Jones, who were merging rap, electro and yob-rock into a kind of beery SF musical party. They used a lot of movie and musical samples, and without thinking too much about it, we started sampling too. Mark was all for it and we found some cool stuff from movies like *Aliens*. This was clearly about as far away as we could get from The Fish Mark 1 and 2. This album would have absolutely nothing in common with the first album. I'd joined the band and it appeared I'd wrecked the joint.

It was all too much for our drummer Graham, who upped and left, and didn't want to discuss it. He was replaced by Stan, who was in one band, and also the bar manager at the legendary Punter's Club in Fitzroy where people congregated for gigs, confabs, and games of pool. He must have taken time off to tour. Stan and I stuck together and kept each other sane when Mark and Martin were stretching our patience. Socially the group was essentially split into two camps, but onstage it was still 'all for one'. There were still times when the four of us all hit top gear when the Fish could wipe the floor with most of our peers.

The second LP came out late in 1990 and was titled *Fin*, with its meanings – the fishy one, and the French word for 'the end'. I think we all saw the writing on the wall. The reviews were all positive, including some in the UK, where the record seemed to have a mysterious provenance in the sense that some reviewers didn't know we were Australian, and therefore were even more surprised by our often-charming eclecticism. But local interest was a bit worrying even though the reviews were uniformly good.

The record was released by Shock, the company where a few of our friends worked. There was a CD, Cassette (all hail the cassette and its unique ability to tangle and tie) and purple vinyl. It was a solid record without any notable weak spots. But Mark wrote sleeve notes without consulting anyone and they were horrible. Twee, and cute, with childish illustrations. All the things I didn't like much about the way the band promoted themselves years beforehand had been repeated.

(The same thing had happened with a T Shirt which arrived out of nowhere in boxfuls, with the name of the band hand-scrawled into a large bubble emerging from the mouth of a badly-drawn Fish. Again, the whole thing was cack-handed and infantile. And I knew nothing about it.)

The outer sleeve of the album didn't really work, and that was probably my fault, as I'd sent a few designs to an old girlfriend and graphic artist and my mock ups weren't up to scratch, but at least it looked modern. Sometimes better ideas only come to you in hindsight.

Gary, who still looked after Melbourne affairs, was none the wiser about Mark's unilateral decisions, but Gary was a good influence, and a circuit breaker if there was trouble. He took the time to listen to my gripes, and to understand how my ups and downs mentally sometimes affected the band. When Mark and I moved out of our flat I lived in Gary's office for a while, which was uncomfortable but psychologically easier.

Moving was something I did with a prolific and yet unavoidable frequency. Gary's place was too small so I secured a small and old flat in Collingwood. After about a month in this tatty unit, a note was slipped under the door to say that the whole building was to be gutted and renovated. I managed to get a similar place across the road, where I lived next-door to a pair of alcoholics who tore the plumbing apart. Not long after that, junkies kicked open all the units to rob them. When they smashed my door down, they were confronted by me. They looked at me and I looked at them, like two species of wildlife presented with a strange new foe, sizing up the possibility of dinner, then they did a runner. Fortunately, I made sure I got the rego number of the stolen car they were using, and after a hearty slap on the back from the cops for my citizenry, the villains were soon caught.

(These moves between houses/flats became even more frequent in the '90s. I've lived, if I include the house where I was born, in thirty different places. Dad and Mum clocked up four each.)

We (the Fish) did appear on Countdown Revolution, which was a slightly paler and less influential version of the 'classic' and for all its sins, unmissable, Countdown. The reboot though was destined to fly well below the radar. And our moment was all over in three minutes.

Mind you, the experience was made a little more bizarre than expected when the hosts Mark Little and Tania Lacy walked out in protest because there wasn't enough 'revolution' on display. As you might expect for a program screened at 6 pm, pushing the envelope wasn't really on the ABC's mind. Little roped in a mandarin from Actors' equity to lean on us and get our support, but we took one look at the remarkable set that the art department had constructed for us, and decided he was too Little (he spat when he talked) and too late. To the broadcaster's credit, about five years later, Recovery appeared. The kind of chaotic vibe and fairly dangerous guests which Little had wanted was now on show. But this was early on a Saturday morning. Not a timeslot when your grandparents would be tucking into a TV dinner.

So now our TV legacy is on YouTube. A dusty relic from a distant epoch. Like my entire career in rock, the message is, 'If you look hard enough, you might be able to see it.'

21

At Christmas the group was essentially off duty but Mark, Martin and I were all in Tasmania, and decided to embark on another side-project, the badly-monikered Wet Spot. We roped in Martin's friend Richard to play bass – he was good – and Richard roped in his friend Lofty to drum – he was short – and we set out to throw everything but the kitchen sink into a setlist with no rhyme or reason. I programmed Martin's drum machine with the beats to about three Pop Will Eat Itself songs and a few Jesus and Mary Chain numbers. (Lofty would sit these ones out.) We'd mix Ramones songs in with Velvet Underground ballads and Roy Orbison and Cheap Trick, and ah, fuck it, just chuck that one in too. Shall we use a megaphone? Why not?

The drum programming was arduous as these were the days when you were 'flying blind' in the sense that there was no visual guide to where you were in the song. Every beat had to be entered manually. Once I'd finished punching in the data, I then had to record each song onto a VHS Tape which we'd cue up, hopefully accurately, and then play through the PA. Amazingly this hope-for-the-best approach worked pretty well. It would only have taken one slight mistake or one badly copied bar of drums and the whole thing would have fallen in a heap.

After the first of our two shows in Hobart I met a girl called Angela, who was completely puzzled by the whole thing. She liked, and owned, all the songs we played but couldn't understand what anyone was doing throwing them all into a lucky dip. I was glad someone had felt it necessary to question what the hell it was we thought we were doing. I didn't really have a proper answer.

Angela was funny and gorgeous, but also nineteen. I was

twenty-eight, so the fact that her parents weren't impressed when she and I began seeing one another was understandable, although if I was forty-five and she was thirty-five, nobody would have blinked. These long-distance relationships had been the norm for me since Andrea moved to Hobart from Launceston in 1982. Later on, I would have partners who lived in Geelong, Sydney, Perth, Castlemaine and Werribee as well as Mentone, which is actually suburban Melbourne, but feels like a strange town in the middle of nowhere.

Angela wrote a phenomenal number of letters to me and I wrote back when I could, and we'd talk on the phone, probably while she was simultaneously writing a letter to me. There were mixtapes, presents. The internet killed all this. It killed the anticipation of the postie arriving. Eventually it was indeed the fact that Angela was still a flighty teenager not yet ready to embrace adulthood that did it for us. It was a shame. I imagine she's middle-aged now.

In April 1991 the band supported the Church at the Hobart City Hall. The hall was large, rectangular and old, so it reminded me of that afternoon in 1978, when the gods smiled on my first ever public performance back at college. The place was full, so I imagine there were more people there than at that school assembly, but of course there was no great thrill in opening for The Church, and not being the reason everyone was there, even though the crowd loved us just fine.

Not long after, we supported the Violent Femmes at The Palace in St Kilda, to what I imagine was a similarly-sized audience, except in a shiny beer barn. Considering the various bands we'd all been in who had played their songs, nobody really made an effort to 'hang out' with the Femmes. They had a room on the opposite side of the stage to us, so that was that pretty much. We punched it hard that night. For all the strange eclecticism which still seeped into The Fish songs, that was a night where I could feel we were surfing on a wave of very high energy. We pushed ourselves to the limit. Physically and mentally. We wanted everyone to remember us as much as The Femmes.

22

Juke was struggling to survive in opposition to the free street press which was now embedded in every major city. There were two magazines in Melbourne; Beat and InPress, and two as well in Sydney; Drum Media and On The Street. All these papers were stuffed with ads placed by venues pushing for that week's line-up. The editorial was pretty good, and included pieces on touring international bands. The idea of paying for a paper which was less comprehensive than one you could collect from the bar of the local pub, or at a record store, for free seemed silly. Juke folded after struggling on until 1992. I had a friend in Sydney who had become editor of On The Street so I began writing for a paper in a different city. This was still pre-internet times, so I had to fax articles (I presume) or did I actually post them in a post box?

The trajectory of The Fish began to assume the slow descent I'd feared. Crowds were down, although we were still forced to tour with Weddings because of our sharing the same hopeless manager. Our own headline shows were sometimes very poorly attended. I wondered whether I killed the band, but without me there wouldn't have been a second album, or a number of successful tours. We just lost momentum and then there was the dagger blow of the Mushroom incident.

Michael Gudinski, who was by far the most influential figure in Australian music, wanted to sign us and apparently a contract was being prepared. Then he got wind that our manager was *that guy* and the offer was withdrawn before it was made. A major label reboot would have meant a flashy video, bigger gigs, more time and money with which to record. Again I may well have wondered how I managed to bluff my way onto a level occupied by 'proper' bands, but I'd have hardly said no.

When the Mushroom deal fell through, I told the others that I was done. No-one was that surprised, and Mark had no intention of fiddling with the line up any more. He was the only original member and his original vision had been skewed by line-up changes and his difficulties trying to write as prolifically as he had a few years earlier.

One of our last gigs seemed to sum the situation up. Somebody booked us to play a car auction in a massive hangar in West Melbourne. I think there were a few bands playing. When we arrived the place was full of buyers and browsers and sellers. It wasn't long though before the cars had vanished, as had the entire crowd (who in any case would have ignored us) we ended up playing to – literally – a man and his dog. It's a shame there aren't photos.

The last ever show was at The Club, where I had spent so many happy nights watching bands when I was young and feckless. The room was maybe half-full. After we'd played our last song, Mark, without warning decided to play a song solo. Maybe it was just vanity or maybe I should have let him have the last word in a band he formed back in Launceston. I just watched him do his thing anyway.

After the demise of the group, I kept busy by moving again, to a share house in Richmond with Bronwyn, the girlfriend of Andrew (who now lived in Tassie) as well as a music nerd, splendidly called Norman. I was in fairly poor health and the whole of 1992 was pretty much a wipe-out, rescued only partially by two Prince gigs.

I wonder what it must have been like to be Prince. You can walk on the moon, discover gravity, paint the Sistine Chapel, but being Prince would have been REALLY crazy. Imagine having music coursing through you so effortlessly. Hearing a song in your head and being able to record it by yourself. Imagine playing a concert for two hours, then going to a club and playing for *another* two hours. RRR had a competition to rename Prince who was at that time officially known as Love Symbol #2, Artist Formerly Known As. The winning name was Davo.

23

At the end of 1992 with nothing happening in Melbourne other than me struggling to pay the rent, and sitting around listening to Matthew Sweet and Teenage Fanclub, I decided to return to Launceston. My friend Sue's parents ran a roadhouse with a large flat at the back which I moved into. But only long enough to learn how to sell petrol and bad sunglasses as a rent subsidy. Then I moved again, naturally. This time to a share unit with Sue below the house of her friend Jerryl near the CBD. There was an open fire in my room which has to be the best antidepressant there is. Pure hypnotic bliss. That tremendous challenge to get the fire started with slightly damp wood and fifteen newspapers. And there was a bath. And an enviable view. Launceston is so full of undulations and micro-valleys that it's difficult to find anywhere *without* a view.

I quickly met a lot of people although most were a fair bit younger than me. It was easy to go out. Nothing was more than five minutes away. It was easy to meet girls, because everyone knew everyone. It seemed everyone at the time was obsessed with Wayne's World. There would be gatherings at our place to watch it, and also a video I had with more Wayne and Garth from Saturday Night Live. The various catchphrases were bandied about and worn smooth from overuse. I don't think anything had affected the zeitgeist as much since Twin Peaks. (Twin Peaks was as unmissable to the Melbourne cognoscenti as a royal wedding is to royalists.)

I re-established myself at the Royal Oak Hotel, scene of many long drinking sessions in the '80s, where one beery night, I ran into an old friend Alex, who I'd known from local bands, and who had also come home from NSW due to lack of opportunity and funds. We decided we should form a band, so we did.

This was going to be a very different affair. Alex played hard and fast and kept it simple, in keeping with his personality. He had a bogan accent, a bogan dog, bogan car, bogan jokes, a bogan vocabulary and yet was somehow not really a bogan. His favourite TV show was *Rugrats*. He surfed and had the regulation long blonde hair. I didn't surf but I had the hair. Alex was in a popular band called Fridge who were in recess and he only knew major chords. I had to teach him about minors and sevenths. He seemed surprised there was more to this whole music business than he'd imagined, and I sensed he knew that a door had been opened for him to more fully exploit his talents, because as a rock guitarist he was more gifted than he might have imagined.

Rod, the drummer in the Outstanding Amount was free so he jumped onboard. Welcome to the world of Lust In Space. Every time we practised we had to haul our gear up a flight of metal outdoor stairs to a second floor room. It was insane. These days, faced with that kind of vertigo-inducing trip, I would simply can the entire project. Initially we bashed out covers by Husker Du, Iggy Pop, Buffalo Tom, Status Quo, The Godfathers, Cheap Trick (naturally) and Kiss. Nothing which required much finesse. I was writing a lot of songs and we added those one at a time. It all came together pretty rapidly and soon enough we were ready to go.

We played our first show at the local 'alternative' pub and it was packed. We sounded huge. I loved the sheer brute force of the sound and the thick hot air and sweat of seething bodies.

Within a few months I'd written a dozen songs and a vacancy came up at the local college recording studio, where students learned how to be sound engineers. So we made an album. The influences were quite specific, but happily, not really obvious; PJ Harvey, Nirvana, John Lennon, the MC5, Redd Kross, Mott The Hoople, Crazy Horse. I tended to write a song and then realise afterwards that I'd subliminally channeled a bit of this or that. Alex used to power-drill his way through all the songs, so the lot of them had a touch of The Stooges too. Essentially my leanings towards pop and glam were fed through Alex's proto-grunge aggression and the two forms welded together well.

We worked at a furious pace, with an old hippie called Jolly, who never said much, but ripped out an enormously energetic sound. Alex struggled with some of the guitar parts so I took over. Being the kind of guitarist that actual guitarists would laugh at I still managed to pull out a few uncomplicated licks (as we musos say.)

I'd written a song called 'Wilson' which was one of those freakish flukey moments when it all comes together. It was clearly the best song, or the best pop song at least, on the record, and would give us an ideal entry point when it came to selling the record to a company.

Not long after we'd finished the LP, I flew to Melbourne to spruik what we'd created to Shock. The boss, David Williams, was so impressed he called in some other label heads to listen. He offered us a deal straight away. The record was going to come out on the Current label (Current as in NOW and also Current as in ELECTRIC … very witty) which was a label where Shock placed their melodic guitar bands (to be vague about it.) The recording had been free and Shock would pay for manufacture and distribution. And they signed us for two more LPs.

We also inked a publishing deal, which was all about collecting royalties, and if anyone had tried hard enough, getting some of our music onto TV shows and films, but I'm not sure that ever happened. Apparently, enquiries were made by a US/UK label called Caroline about getting the overseas rights, but I was only reminded of this when I delved back into the scrapbook I kept at the time. I must follow that up with the guy who signed us, who still has a label in Melbourne

I returned to Tasmania to break the news about Shock and we kept gigging. I wrote reviews for the local paper, just to get free records really, and help out Rod Smith the music editor who I'd become friends with.

We played at another Basin Concert, in early 1994. It was cool to perform an entire set of original material. Not such a big deal for most acts, but rare for a local group. Unfortunately, the onstage carpet hadn't been secured and taped properly and at one point my feet went from under me and I landed hard on my back, slamming my head into the stage. It seemed best to continue playing, which I did until someone pushed me upright like a mannequin and the show went on. We may have recorded these songs, but a few had never been played live before, so it wasn't the most accurate hour of music we'd performed. Rod excelled however, so if Alex and I wandered into unknown territory, Rod would haul us back.

It was fairly obvious now that Lust in Space would have to set up home base in Melbourne. These 'to and fro' moves across Bass Strait were second nature to me now but I still hated them. I found another place to stay, lord knows how. I remember I was sharing with two girls, but I have no idea how I knew them. Rod had a burgeoning family and a pregnant burgeoning wife and there was no way he was going to be able to make the trip. Phil the drummer in Fridge took over. Those guys were scattered all over the place and I don't think they knew when they'd re-convene. Over the next few years, I don't recall Alex and Phil ever not being able to play or tour due to Fridge commitments. Phil was a hell of a drummer, an absurdly good-looking man, and a complete enigma who rarely said much at all.

Most of my Melbourne friends, and friends of friends came to our first show at The Punter's Club. It was a good start and everything augured well. The album, *Glamnesia* was released in mid-1994. The reviews were positive, verging on gushing, except for one guy who liked it, but thought it was a bit muddled. It *was* muddled too. That's how I fly dude! In Rolling Stone, the often-caustic Mark Demetrius seemed to temporarily lose his marbles. He wrote that we 'kicked like a mule' on *Glamnesia*, and that it had an 'exquisite balance of historical perspective and sparkling freshness which characterises the purest rock & roll.' Crumbs. He went on to compare us to the Sex Pistons and The Beatles, saying that we played without cliche and that that was rare to find these days, especially in glam/hard rock, and even more so when it was 'imbued with wit and intelligence.'

The review was so unexpected and almost embarrassing, that it made news in itself. Interviewers would ask us what we thought about the review rather than the record itself. It may also have created the kind of hype that's impossible to live up to. Had we had more time to work on the arrangements for *Glamnesia* it may have been far better, a little more like the Redd Kross album *Phaseshifter* which was what everyone was listening to. It's possible though, being my own harshest critic, that I was nitpicking and that we'd pretty much nailed it as far as saying 'Here we are.'

Unfortunately for Alex, a few months later, the same guy reviewed the first Fridge EP and absolutely slapped it into next week.

24

Gigs came thick and fast, both headliners and supports. We didn't really mind where we were on a bill, as long as the other bands were simpatico. Unlike the Fish, with the gruelling drives, Lust In Space concentrated on Melbourne's inner-city; Fitzroy, Collingwood, North Melbourne, St Kilda. At that time there were multiple venues in all these suburbs. The relationship between the bands was more symbiotic than combative, with punters moving from one pub to the next throughout the night like restless ghosts, pale, etiolated dressed in black.

Then someone stole my bass guitar. I was parked – I had a car? What kind of car? Who gave me a car? – outside my friend Jo's house. I didn't lock the car after a gig, and the rest was inevitable. The kind of self-loathing you feel when you've done something so unutterably stupid is so powerful you wonder if you'll ever get over it. The guitar cost me six-hundred dollars, and was worth a few thousand. I remained a mediocre musician but my bass, which had a thing called an 'active pick-up' was a gem. Anyone could pull a good sound on it, even if you were hitting the strings with a spoon.

I remember bursting into Jo's bedroom where she was in bed with her boyfriend, and saying "Someone's stolen my bass!" as though the two of them might jump out of bed and get cracking on the case. But it was gone. It never came home. A friend of mine ran a guitar shop, so naturally I warned him that someone might try to sell the bass to him, and at the same time I bought another bass. The only way to forget about this calamity was to find a new guitar to play around with and explore. But I still grieve for that stolen guitar.

The mid-'90s are viewed by many now – well, me anyway – as a golden age for independent music and I can tell you why. it was the last decade before every sound seemed to be digitally created, digitally, enhanced, digitally processed or digitally altered, and not with any degree of subtlety – the 2010s especially saw the rise of the machines, the emergence of AI tuned vocals, and a lot of very, very fey and irritating bands. There are of course exceptions, but the JJJ Hot 100 makes me weep.

So now, when a good one does come along, as they can still do now and then, the shock is quite something. If Lust In Space were pushing music to kids in 2022 we would be wildly out of sync, even though some of the bands we shared bills with in 1994, like Spiderbait (who I never liked to be honest) are still doing their thing. Jack White is stronger post-White Stripes than he was two decades ago, and Liam Gallagher just keeps doing the same old shit, but quite well. Whether that means fifty-five year-olds are still buying their records, I don't know. (The most interesting music being made as I write is by female bands and solo artists; Aldous Harding, Wet Leg, Haim, Warpaint, The Linda Lindas, Caroline Polachek, First Aid Kit, Dua Lipa, Olivia Dorigo, Britney Carlile, Beyonce, Band Maid, Taylor Swift.)

Britpop became a blanket term for an explosion of acts who formed in the early '90s and hit their peaks a few years later. I was immediately seduced by the whole thing, but the pre-eminent figures, as far as the press were concerned – Blur (middle class) and Oasis (working class) – were less compelling to me than the bands who didn't seem to have one foot stuck in the '60s. I became a big fan of Pulp (geeky), Suede (posh), Supergrass (playful) and Manic Street Preachers (political) and to a lesser extent, Lush (lush.) Some might argue the movement, such as it was, began with the Smiths and Stone Roses, but there was a narrative to fulfill and papers to sell.

There were peripheral bands like Elastica, Sleeper,

Catatonia, Ash, Stereophonics and Denim. It has to be said though that for a game-changer in music, the lifting was done by only a few bands who became very, very big. And the first rule of Britpop was to claim you weren't Britpop, as all the Britpop bands insisted on reminding us. It was hard to see that amongst this embarrassment of riches that anybody would say that their favourite band were the deeply average Catatonia.

It's easy to assume that decade was dominated by Blur and Oasis, and to a lesser extent, the other prominent bands and their classic singles, but none can be found in the top 20 hits of the '90s in the UK. You can however find the Teletubbies at number seventeen. Even Pulp's 'Common People' which rose to number two, momentarily, struggled to make the cut in the top forty selling songs of 1995, and was kept from the summit by a deplorable version of 'Unchained Melody' by two mediocre TV actors.

Alex, and Phil (I presume) had no interest in this quite English and rather *too* flashy stuff, and I too, even as an avid listener, wasn't really being influenced by these bands musically. We had our own furrow to plough, and continued, with each new song, to play to our strengths.

Lust In Space had none of the tensions of the Fish. It was peculiar but Alex and I were quite protective of one another, and enjoyed each other's company. He had his moments with the 'black dog' and we could share these. Phil was so mysterious he didn't seem to be either very happy or very annoyed by anything. Perhaps we should have taken the next step and asked him to be completely silent, like Stan Laurel or Teller from Penn and Teller. It might have been a selling point.

With Shock's money and a handful of new songs, Lust In Space returned to Whirled to record again. The songs had more layers and I recruited Martin to record a few acoustic guitar parts which were a bit beyond Alex's 'Mr Rock' remit. Artists always seem to remember where they were when they wrote songs. I don't remember these at all, and I don't remember teaching them to the band. They seemed to pop up when we got to Whirled, fully formed. We decided to cover Cheap Trick's 'Surrender' which was a pretty dumb move. The song was already a kind of alternative-rock standard. We added nothing to the original, and played it far, far too slowly. I have no idea why.

It didn't come naturally to me to write power-rock/pop with the emphasis on power, because mostly I'd recorded demos by myself on cheap gear with barely any amplification which resulted mostly in dreamy and intimate tunes. Writing for a rock band necessitated a change of direction, but fortunately it didn't mean I had to jettison melody or the little tricks in chord changes, most of which I'd learnt from other songs. The 5-Track EP was called *Speed Queen*. It was named after a washing machine. But sounded sexy.

Whirled was a bit of a rabbit warren, so don't be thinking we'd arrived at Abbey Road. The control room was about half the size of a regular lounge and the studio itself was a little smaller. Craig, the engineer had all the state-of-the-art gear we needed, but there was no room for a pool table or any other distractions from the often-tiresome process of listening and listening again and listening again.

David at Shock wasn't quite as thrilled with *Speed Queen*, as he had been with *Glamnesia*. It was probably better, but there was nothing with quite the instant bite that 'Wilson' had, and the opening track (and radio generally plays track one) had a very long drum intro, so we didn't get to the meat and potatoes of the song for a little while. We could have edited the song. That would have been easy enough, but that, strangely, didn't occur to anyone at the time.

So we launched the record, and toured Tassie and played a lot in Melbourne and maintained a kind of mid-level indie popularity, but commercial radio didn't come near us, and we didn't really have the money to make a video. If we had made a video, it may well have had little effect on sales, but what if it *had* a very large effect? It would have been the best investment, we, and Shock could have made, but it never happened.

Our most notable support was when we opened for US rockers Urge Overkill. Of all our contemporaries (if a contemporary means a band who existed in a time frame and looked way cool) Urge were the band I was most impressed with after they released the *Saturation* album in 1993. They seemed to be heavily influenced by Cheap Trick and came flaming out of the post-grunge era with flair, matching clothes and guitars and an endless repository of riffs and catchy melodies. *Saturation* is probably the most underrated rock album of all time and was clearly getting a spin when bands like The Hellacopters and Tassie heroes Devilrock Four were formulating their attack. Urge Overkill's biggest hit was a cover of Neil Diamond's 'Girl You'll Be a Woman Soon.' Which appeared on the *Pulp Fiction* soundtrack. Their LPs had fantastically glamourous names; *Jesus Urge Superstar*, *Americruiser*, and *The Supersonic Storybook*. It's no coincidence that I decided on *Glamnesia* (and Lust In Space.)

Unfortunately Urge Overkill were diabolically bad live. Bad enough for people to pen letters of complaint to the street rags afterwards. I had my copy of their LP signed by the guitarist Eddie 'King' Roeser, and he was clearly wasted. It was all a bit sad really. They'd been on tour with Nirvana and it's possible they may have been partying a little too hard with Kurt who was in the grip of heroin addiction. Before the lawyers come knocking, I should say I'm speculating here.

This was the time too when I started to fantasise about programming Rage. Forcing my favourite songs and film clips down other people's throats sounded perfect for me. We just weren't big enough to be asked. The artists who were programming Rage were picking terrible songs (in my mind of course), or cliched songs, (and I'm looking at everyone who has selected '(I'm) Stranded' by the Saints.) These days I'm even more mystified by the choices. Millennial bands pick the songs of other millennial bands and don't seem to understand that music didn't begin in 2000.

As well as being invisible to the important folks at Rage, there was also a worrying lack of action in Sydney. As I was the default manager of Lust in Space, it was up to me really, but we needed a solid contact in Sydney, or agency representation. I organised every gig we played. Alex had become lazier and lazier, and Phil was like a wraith. I was working full time on booking shows and promoting the record. Bear in mind there was still no internet (not for home use anyway) and therefore no email, and the phone was glued to the wall (and my ear.) My weapons were photocopiers, textas and rulers. UHU Sticks, scissors and old books I'd chop to bits to make flyers.

So on we ploughed, at The Punters Club, The Evelyn, The Public Bar, The Prince Of Wales, The Empress, The Nicholson, The Esplanade, The Armadale. One night at a small pub in Fitzroy we were booked to play before a band from New South Wales I'd never heard of. During our set the place got more and more crowded. But not with a normal rock crowd. These people were kids. Kids with their parents in many cases. By the time we'd finished – having been ignored for an hour – you could barely move. And then on came silverchair. Even then I was none the wiser about who silverchair were, but obviously they were already some sort of teeny-grunge phenomenon, led by a pretty boy singer/guitarist and two average blokes who'd lucked in.

This fervid vibe, this air of excitement, was not something I'd been privy too before. Like Beathoven, long before, silverchair had conquered arguably the most important demographic of all. Teenage girls. News of a group with a cute young singer would spread like Covid in the schoolground. Never, ever underestimate the power of young women to dictate who makes it and who doesn't.

One night at the Public Bar after we'd done our thing, a quite spectacular tall and striking blonde approached me and started to chat. I was a bit confused. Did she think I was someone else? She didn't seem to have the slightly over-the-top vibrations it was possible to spot in what, for want of a better word, was a 'groupie'. Her name was Alex. She was a physic lecturer, ex-model – Big M being one of her TV ads – and a gifted competitive swimmer. The other Alex kept looking over and pulling faces at me, of the 'you have got to be shitting me' kind. Alexandra was chatty, a bit odd. She laughed a lot and was free of cynicism. She seemed to be an unusually well-balanced and happy person.

One thing quickly led to another, and although she lived in Geelong, I would drive down now and then, and she'd come up now and then. What you saw was what you got. She wasn't wry, or witty, but she had a great record collection and was always smiling. It was puzzling. I was a classic commitment-phobe and was never convinced Alexandra was entirely right, and then she confessed that she had a kind of casual boyfriend already who was being a hit clingy and when she met me she thought she'd end it with him, but she hadn't, not properly.

It made sense for us to, at the least, take a break, but then I met an English girl called Alison when I was playing pool one night, and I realised it was time to move on. I kept in touch with Alexandra in the 2010s when her health wasn't great. She died of cancer about five years ago. I'd never known a friend to die.

25

The band were invited to contribute a song to a Go-Betweens tribute CD, and I was pleased to discover that no other bands had chosen 'Apology Accepted' or 'Part Company', both of which I'd always liked. We decided to merge the two tracks. I wedged the riff of 'Part Company' into the middle of 'Apology Accepted'. It was a bit of a tricky weave with an unusual time signature, and it baffled Alex, so I played the 'fiddly' bits. Anna (of 'Michael Told Me' fame) added some backing vocals and put me to shame. I should have asked her to sing lead vocals.

The rest of the bands who took part were pretty much like us: all of them had released albums and none of them were especially famous. Frente were probably the biggest band, The best musically, the one with real pedigree, were The Black Eyed Susans who had Triffids connections and a vocalist in Mark Snarski who had a god-given gift for a ballad.

I was sharing a huge house in Richmond with Anna, Kiernan from the Black Eyed Susans, Kirsty who worked at Shock and a guy called Richard, who Anna described as an 'Energy Vampire'. I wonder now how I managed to feel so relaxed in share houses where complications and personal quirks should, by rights, create tensions. Anna and I would have long rambling talks into the early hours. She was away now and then, touring, most notably as back-up singer for Grant McLennan from the Go-Betweens. Who cooked? Did they cook for everyone? Who cleaned, vacuumed, swept?

After a year or so Anna bought a house, then Kirsty and Phil from the Susans bought a house too and I think Kiernan may have moved in with a girlfriend, so once again I found a unit of my own.

The momentum of the band was slowing as was the interest of Alex (and probably Phil.) We played a few not-so-great gigs and the mood in the band room at the last one was completely miserable. I asked Alex if he was done with it and he said he was, and that was that. I think he just wanted to go surfing. He walked out of the pub and I didn't see him for eight years.

So another band had more or less petered out rather than split for more memorable reasons such as drugs, fights, Yoko Onos, fatal plane crashes, or choking on vomit. Lust In Space hadn't really got past the laying-groundwork phase. Ultimately it was dispiriting, but like The Fish, there were the records. There was posterity of a kind.

I secured a job at Shock, writing bios for new releases. It was a good gig, although some of the records were not to my taste. I was forced to make almost everything seem like the greatest release since *Abbey Road*. Eventually you just run out of breathless adjectives when describing a band from Canada whose bio adjectives might actually be best described as 'inoffensive' or 'pedestrian.'

Later I shifted downstairs to the warehouse and became one of the drones who picked CDs from shelves to make up orders. Stacking CDs up your arm from wrist to shoulder was an invitation to disaster, but all of us became so expert at balancing large quantities of discs we could have formed a circus troupe.

The number of Shock employees who played in bands was almost comical. If you *didn't* play in a band you were a little anomalous. I had decided that Lust In Space was only on hold, so technically I was in a band. If you want to know why I stopped working at Shock … so do I. I simply don't remember.

My disappointment about the band's (partial) demise was alleviated somewhat by my finally breaking down the defences of Lisa who had resisted my attempts at flirting without appearing to be flirting for several years. We would meet up to drink and play pool and were good friends and I imagine she knew I would have liked something more. She gave me a lot of lifts home from pubs and never came in for a 'euphemism' coffee, and then one night she kissed me. I'm not sure *why*, but, in any case we entered into a proper grown up relationship.

We liked the same bands, mostly, shared a sense of humour which was fired by the questionable, tasteless and cruel. I was able to be myself and never have to ask 'Who *is* this person? Are they wondering who I am?' We were equally comfortable staying in and playing scrabble, or attending gigs. Even after a fairly solid year, neither of us really considered moving in together, which said something but I'm not sure what, except I'd never lived with a girlfriend and wasn't sure I knew how to do it. Lisa still lived in the family home with her Mum and she seemed happy enough there. Were we inseparable? Not really? Did we enjoy time alone? Yes. And I realise I had stayed in many share houses. This would have been quite different and it barely came up in conversation.

Martin had had a sort of depressive breakdown and urged me to move in with him in his terrace house in North Fitzroy. I wasn't the absolute ticket myself, and had had a stint at the Melbourne Clinic, with some ECT treatment. (I know this may seem important, and it is, but not to this particular story.) Martin told me later that my being there helped him get through (with medication) the worst of it, even though it felt at the time like I was merely irritating him.

Without a band and with the journalism having dried up it was the most barren time I'd spent in Melbourne. But having not learned my lesson, soon enough I was in negotiations with friends and formulating another group to start from scratch. I must have been mad.

David Dixon was nuts. If things weren't going fast enough for him, and you'd think they were if you met him, he'd take drugs to make them go faster. He had no pause button, definitely no stop button, and probably eschewed the play button and went straight to fast forward. He never had a girlfriend because of all the other girlfriends he had. I presumed

David was priapic because he seemed to want sex all the time. He told me he'd felt it necessary to take Viagra one night and became so aroused he started to have thoughts about Marge Simpson. He didn't drive, because he was drunk a lot, and probably never calmed down long enough to learn. So I had to drive him everywhere. David had played guitar in a band called Nursery Crimes when he was younger. God knows how insufferable the fucker would have been back then.

That band were pretty big. They toured the UK. I'm not sure how to describe them. Speed-glam? They played with their shirts off and had unfeasibly long hair and played guitars that looked like they'd been pilfered from Poison and fed through a Sex Pistols filter. They did a manic version of 'Eleanor Rigby'.

We were fortunate to recruit an old member of the Tasmanian crew Gary Aspinal who I'd been recording with. He did a nice turn in making his guitar sound like various other instruments. He also enjoyed drugs and was in a relationship with Anna, and not surprisingly played in The Killjoys too, adding to a more conventional pop sound. Being a member of several bands was never unusual for the broad coterie of music contacts I had. Graham from the Fish agreed to drum.

David's voice was stronger than mine, and we included a handful of his songs, all of which he sang, along with some new ones of mine, a few Lust In Space numbers and a couple of Power Pop classics; 'Girl Of My Dreams' by Bram Tchaikowsky and 'Serious Drugs' originally by Cobain favourites, BMX Bandits.

Again I found myself in charge of finding gigs, sifting through a list of possible names for the band, and organising practices. I decided and nobody really cared one way or another that we should be called Zero 2 Sixty.

Our first show at The Club was a catastrophe. Gary was stoned on something and instead of playing the songs, opted for an admixture of my Bloody Valentine and Pink Floyd. This threw the rest of us off kilter, until it seemed like we were all playing the wrong song.

Graham left the band soon after he'd packed up his kit. I had no choice, it seemed to me at least, to show Gary the door too. He was unimpressed but I'm not sure I had a choice, other than to put the whole project in a box labelled 'never to be opened', and sliding it into an attic somewhere. But naturally I did some more recruiting. James was a guitar freak who taught the instrument and could play the lead break of every AC/DC song to order … except I didn't need him for that. He was ten times funnier than anyone I've ever known, and didn't even try. It made him excellent company. Our new drummer, Frank, played in a band called Moondriven with some friends of mine (and David's sister.)

We rebooted as Jacuzzi Suit, the name borrowed from a contraption worn by Millhouse's mother in The Simpsons. Mark from the Premier booking agency found us a few shows, as he had sporadically with Lust In Space. We played about a gig per month for a year or so, but all of them were forgettable. We had no particular selling points. It was a bit of a hotch-potch of indifferent songs, although we did manage to do a radio session on the independent station 3RRR, where we covered Bowie's 'Ashes To Ashes' reasonably well, even though it was never in our set. I don't recall that we definitively split up. Frank may have been busy with other commitments; bar work, Moondriven, punching bouncers (he was not a man to cross.) And at that stage James was teaching full-time, so again it was only really me who had the time for it.

In case you're wondering why I hadn't moved lately … I had, to Caulfield with Phil from Nursery Crimes and his former girlfriend Michelle. I'd concluded that Martin and I couldn't pursue the sharing situation, and he was stronger mentally too. But of all my possibly unnecessary upheavals, this was probably the worst. Michelle ensured me she wasn't a junkie any more, but she was. That's enough to make a house both miserable and somehow squalid. Now and then touring rock stars would mysteriously drop by, so Michelle had a bit of a business going.

Like all heroin users there was actually an okay person in there somewhere. She spent hours in the expansive garden, making ours the most impressive in the street. She enjoyed cooking, and I got on fine with Phil. But after six months or so, I had to get out. Michelle was furious. So much so that I needed a police escort to pack my car in some sort of safety. She decided she'd tell the landlord, who lived next door, but my name wasn't on the lease, so that was pretty futile.

Farewell Caulfield, hello East Brunswick.

26

Lisa and I were together (sometimes) and untogether (at other times) and it was all a bit messy, and it was probably my fault because of mood swings. We did work together for a time at a primary school where she was in charge of the after-school care program. A vacancy came up as her assistant and she dragged me in without the school doing any kind of checks on me. I hasten to add, I would have come up squeaky clean, but what if I was some kind of mild-mannered monster, just waiting for an opportunity like this?

I had to be there at about 7 am. Sometimes I'm sure I would have stayed up, hungover, and not welcomed 8-year-olds shouting at me as the painful morning sunlight screamed through the windows. I'd have an afternoon nap and return to school at about 3 pm. I enjoyed the job although my fantasy of instantly having my authority respected was way off beam. I always thought that teaching was something I'd be good at. Now I wasn't so sure. It wasn't that the kids ran amok or beat one another up. I could cut that stuff off. And I was able to organise them into various activities. I just noticed a simmering lack of respect, and a few of the naughtier children liked to push things a little because I wasn't the Headmistress who was respected one-hundred-percent, and who scared me a little too.

Lisa was always a 'good sport' as they say. If I challenged her, she would accept the challenge. A good example was when we went to see the Manic Street Preachers at The Prince Of Wales. Music was in a bit of a vacuum (which wasn't going to be dynamically filled by Pavement or Sebadoh or Beck) while everyone waited for the White Stripes and The Strokes to be invented. The Manics' LP *Everything Must Go* was my go-to listening for about a year. (Eventually they became Martin's favourite band. I tried to *tell* him but he was so stubborn. Then the penny dropped for him.)

The Manic Street Preachers were in some way a band out of time. They might have slotted in to the zeitgeist of 1977 or, who knows, 2027, but in 1998 they had no peers. Sloganeering socialists who were big on grand statements and revolution in the head, they were musically a melodic hard rock band with no trendy aspects of dance or '60s-revivalism in anything they did. They sounded pretty much asexual (unlike, say the sensual Suede) but liked to play around with eye-make-up and feather boas and an androgynous image. No other bands were interested in private angst or unionism or nihilism. The isms were many. The tragic disappearance of their rhythm guitarist Richey Edwards in 1994 added to their myth as the band who would literally die for you.

After the show I dared Lisa to get James from the band to autograph her breast. (This might have been exploitative and titillating if it wasn't Lisa ... but it *was* Lisa.) The Manics were very big on various leftie causes, and probably didn't go round signing the tits of their female fans. They weren't AC/DC. But Lisa worked her charms, or one of them, and signed her boob indeed was. The subsequent blame for this incident has been put firmly at my own feet, which is unfair.

I had a wonderful white cat called Ziggy who had become accustomed to moving house, and seemed to adapt to each upheaval without fuss. The flat in East Brunswick was already his fourth home. Pet therapy is fine and you can fool yourself into thinking your cat (*never* a dog) is an affectionate and gentle soul, until you see it eat a rat from tail to crunchy skull.

There was some sporadic writing work. I submitted a few pieces to a couple of online magazines which had potential but ultimately didn't get a foothold in the burgeoning dog-eat-dog world of the internet. I became the 'male' voice of Australian

Women's Forum, a glossy magazine that still had a hunk of the month centrefold. I wrote about men, for women, and pretended to understand how the male mind worked. A few similar pieces in Cosmopolitan covered similar territory.

There was also a soccer fanzine at that time which I co-edited. I was passionate about the club (Carlton) and, with the Lightning Seeds' 'Four Lions' football-themed hit as an impetus, I wrote a 'soccer song', which in fact was maybe the best thing I'd ever done. I decided it should be recorded, and decided too that it didn't matter who played on it, because the project would be new music from Lust In Space.

I managed to recruit a pretty good band. Martin and Mark (Fish Mark) played the main guitar parts and contributed backing vocals, James from Jacuzzi Suit ripped out a lead break for the main track, Graham from The Fish played drums. We recorded with Craig from The Killjoys. As well as the Carlton song, 'A Dream Won't Do' we also took the opportunity to knock out 'One Of Your Bets' which I'd written in 1987, recorded with Lust In Space in 1996 (on *Speed Queen*) as a kind of homage to Neil Young, and had now re-arranged as a mostly-acoustic ballad. Martin's song 'Bridgitta' which probably should have been on the Fish's *Fin* LP finally got an airing. We used a lot of samples from commentary of games and that worked a treat too.

The novelty of a band recording a CD for their club was catnip for a few TV shows who must have been having slow news weeks. Football Mundial was a magazine television show which was dubbed into hundreds of languages, shown in hundreds of countries, and covered that week's activities in the world game. Football Mundial wanted to do a segment on us. Baffled but naturally intrigued (and also wondering if it might mean a rapid escalation in royalties), Martin and I trundled out to Carlton's training ground to meet with the players and a camera crew. I got to have a kick around with guys like Archie

Thompson which was fun, and not embarrassing since I'd played at a fairly high level in the past. Then I had to choreograph them doing a sort of can-can to the song. After all that, I missed the show, but in an event which eerily echoed the John Peel affair, the father of one of the players, in Brazil, didn't miss it, and there we were, in Portuguese. "Queremos que todos os fãs recebam o cd!"

The song started being played before games at Olympic Park. We sold it by hand a bit like the Big Issue. Carlton got kicked out of the National Soccer League in a travesty of justice, largely the fault of the then owner. For a while the game itself was in disrepair, and was then re-launched as the A League. I supported (and continue to support) Melbourne Victory, but the intimacy of the Carlton days were over.

We were played on radio a little, but the subject matter, to most people other than Carlton supporters, was a little strange. Yet the benefits of undertaking the project were plenty. In the long run we may well have sold more copies of 'A Dream Won't Do' than *Speed Queen*. The song itself was the best I'd ever written, and I would have been happy to play it to Noel Gallagher. But he would have ripped it off.

27

Here I was without a band, or a soccer club, or any journalism on the horizon, or financial security, so I decided it would be a *brilliant* idea to write a novel. I had a vague idea for a story about a struggling musician who was obsessed with game shows, and constantly thwarted in his attempts to get on one and win money. In the real world, I had no money, so it was easy to write about having no money. I was the ultimate armchair expert when it came to quiz shows, and the band thing … well that could write itself. It would a be a *roman a clef*, and there was no point pretending otherwise.

With no prior experience in fiction, my chances of being published appeared to be about zero, but a friend who'd written a few successful chick-lit books when that genre was a new thing, read about six chapters, and urged me to continue. A little later I sent some more to an agent she knew, and although he passed, it was again suggested it was worth finishing the book and sending it to some publishers. So … because I had nothing else to do.

I called the book *Buzzed* and sent it to Penguin. Not long after, I got a phone call inviting me to their offices. Even then I wondered whether they liked to reject submissions personally for maximum disappointment, but no, Penguin wanted to publish the book.

For the next six months or so I was busy re-writing, working with an excellent editor and adding some chapters to *Buzzed* which had previously faded a little in the third act. I had to choose a cover and was sent some pretty bad ones. When Penguin were on the verge of choosing one themselves, they got it right, and it was all systems go. They paid me an advance. It made my eyes water.

I'd run into my old friend Sue, who I'd shared with before, and who was now living in a capacious Edwardian bungalow in Richmond, which had a room available. I was seduced a little by the luxuries of a bath, atrium, large balcony, massive living area and proximity to the MCG. I put the cat in his travel cage and off we went again.

The only problem was that the spare room story was a little mythical. Dan, who had actually designed all the Lust In Space sleeves, was supposed to move out, but his idea of moving out was to do it *sometime*, if he felt like it, if he found somewhere that dropped in his lap, and otherwise he'd stay put, commandeering two large bedrooms, one for his bed and salon selection of shoes, and one for his computer. I was banished to a spare room designed for no more than storage.

This stalemate seemed to last forever, and Dan wasn't exactly sympathetic to my plight. He was often drunk and he was often having arguments with Sue. I'm not sure two people have ever had such a mutually poisonous relationship. If I wasn't in my little cupboard, I was avoiding altercations and fights which I had no dog in. I had no dog anyway.

Buzzed was released and I spent some time feverishly pushing it. I had a gorgeous young girl from Penguin working on publicity who had to convince me that Cabcharge was a thing. What luxury! There were a lot of glowing reviews, feature articles on me/the book, in a variety of newspapers and magazines, as well as several radio interviews one on Melbourne ABC Breakfast.

I soon realised that I was enjoying the kind of media attention (albeit different media) that precisely none of my bands had ever attracted. And it felt like I hadn't had to put much effort into it at all. This was all back to front. I now decided that music had perhaps been a kind of folly, and possibly not even worth the sweat, the road trips, and dealing with loose cannons like Alex and David. It would be churlish to deny that I did meet outstanding and charming people who I certainly wouldn't have met if I had worked in a bank and not played in a band. But 'trappings' would have been nice; a new car, flying everywhere instead of puttering along in a van, invitations to glitzy awards ceremonies … and being fucked asked to fucking program Rage.

Meeting girls by writing books wasn't as likely to happen as meeting girls when they've sidled up to you and said "Hello I really liked your band" in the slightly disinhibited and tipsy atmosphere of a gig, but it seemed sensible to eschew rock'n'roll and start work on novel number two anyway. It wasn't much good, and I realised I might have only had that one fluky book in me. I did have a short story in a compendium collated into a book for charity alongside contributions from people like Nick Hornby, Tara Moss and er … Joan Collins. Again, I had, as the vernacular goes 'pulled that one out of my arse.' The novel was eventually finished, but I knew that it was an inglorious flaming failure. And so did my agent.

Writing one novel after another was clearly something some people managed to do, and I was not going to be one of them. Perhaps it would all mirror my music life after all. Minor triumphs. Greater frustrations. An abject failure to become a household word.

28

In 2002 Brian Wilson returned to Australia for the first time since a Beach Boys tour in 1964. The story is well known; his nervous breakdown, drug freak outs, withdrawal from the world, virtual imprisonment by quack doctor Eugene Landy, and miraculous recovery. His band played the whole of the spectral *Pet Sounds* LP and some more conventional hits.

After the show some friends and I settled in at a club called Cherry, which was our usual destination for a late-night rendezvous, I was bugged by a strange inkling that Wilson's band might have convened at another club which was a little further down the same laneway as Cherry. I'm not sure if anyone ever went there, and I never had, but to satisfy this nagging suspicion I wandered in, and lo, there they were. So I told them that Cherry would be a better bet, with more people and better music – it was soul night – and I led them there. It was slightly spooky to have found them in a club to which I'd never given a second thought.

There were five members of the band, and Jenny, the fiancé of the keyboard player Scott. I wondered if I could get some flirting happening with Taylor, the backing vocalist, but she was married to the drummer in Styx. Styx were a kind of progressive-soft-metal band who were bad for several decades, and apparently hadn't finished yet. Taylor seemed nice though.

I hit it off with Nelson, the band's percussionist, and we've grown closer over the several visits he's made to Melbourne with Brian. When he was in town for the 50th Anniversary of The Beach Boys in 2012, Nelson met my buddy Michael and I and allowed us to sit in on the band's soundcheck, then said we should hang around for some food. This led to the surreal situation of me standing at the bain-marie next to Mike Love, a man I'd gladly have poisoned with the mashed potato for his consistently artless attitude to music, his hindering of the group's progress, his bullying of Brian, his vexatious lawsuits, arrogance and general creepiness.

On their most recent visit Nelson, and Probyn, who plays a bit of everything, sat down with me and talked about Brian for an interview which was published in Australian Musician. They were pretty forthcoming with mildly gossipy stories which was pleasing. So now and then I was still writing. This time about Brian Wilson's habit of not chewing before he swallowed.

The frequency of work increased again when I wrote a piece every month for a few years, for Time Out, about classic Melbourne venues and songs. Even these sporadic articles helped save me from penury. I also reviewed LPs for Beat, which was pro bono work, but did enable me to source free CDs which I would then sell.

I would love to have a list of all the records I used to own. It feels like I still have too many even though I have had enormous clean-outs over the years. Having waxed lyrical earlier on about early Queen, you might be surprised to know I gave *all* my Queen records to a friend presuming I would never be interested in them again. I had to sell a special edition box of The Beach Boys' *Smile* record which featured a 3-dimensional store front and massive poster, just to buy something for dinner. The only way to make money from selling secondhand records is to sell the best ones you own. I have had to push back on this and draw a line. I refuse to sell my original Cheap Trick records for example.

I've had to come to terms with a disaster I suffered when I moved from Melbourne to Launceston (I think.) All my singles were in a box, and the box vanished. Because New Wave was initially a movement dominated by 45s, coloured vinyl, and classic sleeves, I lost many valuable records. It makes me wince to consider what I no longer have. They do say, 'You can't take it with you'. This is no comfort at all.

I was DJing every few Saturdays at Cherry, playing wall-to-wall rock, with occasional dollops of funk and pop. Work began at midnight and ended at 6 am. I liked being in charge, and playing what I wanted, while using a degree of manipulation to keep the dance floor full.

In those days if I needed or wanted songs, I could download them from the net and burn them onto a CD-R. It was a bootlegger's picnic, a digital piracy piss-up, and a peer-to-peer party. I jumped right in. I might have argued, whilst apologising profusely to, let's say, Neil Young, that had there not been free music available to download at that time, I never would have heard *Comes A Time*, or alternatively, I might have bought *On The Beach*, without realising it was rubbish. Anyone who began their magpie ways with Napster and then moved on to P2P, knew that the authorities would arrive to shut things down, and that all that would be left would be the hangover. Downloadable music was made most attractive by its portability. These days I can still find some obscure Sparks tune from 1994, but only as a YouTube stream or on Spotify free which is clumsy. My emphasis here, the point I'm making, is how I'm expert at getting something for nothing, then being not entirely happy with it.

There was another night club I worked at called Control run by local identity Wal Kempton. Control was closer to home, as well as attracting a more interesting crowd, probably due to a kind of membership system, where you got an e-tag which would open the front door. I enjoyed DJing there a lot, but when the smoking laws were toughened up and Wal needed a bouncer downstairs all of a sudden, it was the death knell. The notion of people lighting up *inside* a venue, as we all used to, appears now to be criminally reckless for anybody unwittingly breathing in smoke let alone the smokers.

Due to his music contacts, rather than any crime contacts, Wal scored me a DJing gig for the St Kilda Police at the Esplanade. In anticipation, I did my utmost to have on hand every kind of radio hit I could. There wasn't much I could do about songs I'd never heard of, by acts I'd never heard of, but I thought, foolishly, that I was tooled up with enough music to get by.

So, I started banging out Beyonce, Pink, Britney Spears, Lady Gaga, Shakira, Christina Aguilera, Black Eyed Peas, The Veronicas etc. The music everyone was listening to at the time if they liked commercial dance-pop. No reaction. So I tried more classic funk like Prince, Fatboy Slim, Gloria Gaynor, maybe early Eminem and The Village People (clearly I was struggling by now.) Eventually, policewomen began to approach me and ask for …

"Something we can dance to."

What else do you do with Lady Gaga *except* dance?

"What would you like to hear?"

"Just something we can dance to."

Clearly there was nothing they could dance to in the entire history of pop music. Somewhere out there I presume there was a terrible song that these deplorable people would leap into action for, and they'd dance to it all night, only pausing to refill their Breezers. I never found out what that might have been. And after a few hours, I was past caring.

The Esplanade was also the venue for a more enjoyable evening around that time when I appeared on Rockwiz. It was very early on in the program's history. I think I was a contestant on the third episode. The preliminaries involved each table of punters in the audience nominating a representative to do a quick audition with chief 'brain' Brian Nankervis. That wasn't especially challenging for me and I found myself on a team with Tim Rogers from You Am I and some other guy. Rogers was a very competitive player and fast on the button. I knew all the answers but he was getting in fast. And hogging the spotlight somewhat, as is his wont. Our team was a narrow winner. Rogers then sang 'Stop Dragging My Heart Around' with

Melbourne music stalwart Rebecca Barnard. (Rockwiz gradually became something of a fixture, continuing for more than eleven years and one-hundred and fifty episodes, plus specials like 'Rockwiz Salutes the Melbourne Music Bowl.')

I've often wondered why You Am I have never been able to get a foothold in the US and UK, given that both Jet and The Vines had their moment in the international spotlight. They've had the benefit of a stable line-up whereas The Vines in particular have had a haphazard career with Craig Nicholls often not in a great place mentally. You Am I have sold many more albums in Australia than either of the other bands but overseas has been a bit of a write off. I'm not a huge fan of Rogers' persistent devotion to cowboy hats, open shirts, Elvis suits and jewellery, and his book was baffling, but the band are an institution, arriving in indie rock's golden age in the early '90s and still firing on all cylinders. Put a record on ... any record, and there's no mistaking who it is. Age shall not weary them.

Soon after Rockwiz I was given the green light to be a contestant on The Einstein Factor, which was an ABC show with certain similarities to Hard Quiz, but with more quizzing and less silliness. My special subject was The Beach Boys. I scored thirteen from fourteen, and then did quite well in the general knowledge round to win the game. I progressed to the semi-finals where I was beaten by a guy who knew a lot about the Melbourne Cup, and was a little faster than me when buzzing in during round two. My frustrations about quiz show selections should have been partially assuaged, but I was still having no luck getting a call up for the programs where big money was on offer. I kept goofing off at the auditions. The questions were dumb, the 'exercises' to extract some sort of idea about your personality were deplorable. I couldn't play their games. I came across as weird. Disruptive. Cynical. All pretty accurate really. The surly rock dog refusing to play straight for the man.

29

Sometime in 2006 I was invited to a gig by Graham's nephew, Carl, who had a band called The Devilrock Four. I'd only met Carl once, when I took him to see INXS in 1988. He'd flown from Launceston and he was just a shy kid. I presumed he'd be a shy adult, and I also presumed his band would play tuneless thrash, so I went under sufferance. My god … they were good – bits of Thin Lizzy, Radio Birdman, AC/DC. Carl was a genuine rock-god showman. He was so good at playing his guitar he didn't even have to think about it, and could just concentrate on the 'moves'.

I was flabbergasted. And offered to help them. A guy called James Young who owned Cherry and loved loud fast rock'n'roll had a label so I set up a meeting. The band released a single and LP soon after. I joined them on tour. (I did lights but some places had very shoddy lights.) And waited for global stardom. And waited. I'm not sure why The Devilrock Four didn't really take flight. Did they need a vocalist like Nic Cester from Jet, a frontman like Rob Younger from Birdman? Something was missing, but when they were on fire, it was hard to fathom what that could be. For someone who still hankered now and then for white guys with loud guitars they were catnip.

The band played at a festival in Hobart, coming on directly before Toni Collette's extremely featherweight and uninteresting band. The Lemonheads were next, and having done his set, Evan Dando donned a German Kaiser's helmet and ran around backstage for an hour. Drugs are bad m'kay?

Stand-up comedy was not a pursuit that people who knew me would have expected to constitute my next foray into the world of entertainment. But it made sense to me – in a weird way. Although I had a diffident, bordering on shy, personality, the stage – any stage – had always been a welcoming place, a second home. It seemed perfectly natural to be up there in 1978, and no less inviting in 2007. Sure, there aren't too many similarities in the disparate worlds of comedy and rock, but the two are probably closer than rock is to dramatic theatre or film. Both comedy and live music happen (mostly) in pubs, in front of audiences having a beer and not entirely sure what's in store for them, knowing that things might go horribly wrong.

The reason I wanted to do stand-up was because I found so much of it to be of a very poor quality. And I watched a lot. It was a kind of punishment to have to do research. I'd never been hilarious company, but this was a very regimented and targeted way of delivering pre-prepared humour, and that suited me. Everything was written down and the flabby bits were offcut. I had some sturdy material so I signed on to the Raw competition. A lot of friends came along, and I was unusually relaxed about the whole thing. The pub was full and this helped a lot. If there are two hundred people in a venue and one hundred and eighty laugh, that's a triumph. If there are twenty people and fifteen laugh, it could be seen as a dud set. Especially in a big room. I came second, which was fine because the winner deserved it. I progressed to the next round, or the semis, but was ill and couldn't compete.

I did however start doing Tuesdays at the Comic's Lounge in North Melbourne. The weekends were reserved for 'name' comedians, so I was basically putting down roots and making inroads on quiet nights, but the room was simply way too big for use as anything other than a Bunnings outlet. After a handful of spots, I decided being funny and fresh would take a lot of effort and my efforts at effort were diminishing with age. Had I been twenty and setting out in 'entertainment', comedy would have made sense. But music made sense too when I was young. So that was my choice.

I was back in a new Shock warehouse in 2009 doing what I'd done more than a decade previously. The strain on my back and knees was a little greater and, now that DVDs were the format of choice for TVs and movies, and Shock had moved into that area, stacking a pile between wrist and shoulder was even more precarious.

Never one to take 'retirement' as a serious option, and with a certain amount of encouragement from my friend the-other-Michael, another band emerged, The TV Set. On drums and vocals; Jamie, on guitar; Michael, on the other guitar; Murray, and on bass and vocals, me. Michael was primarily a drummer and would have been an insufferable show off super-musician if not for being such a wonderful and very funny human being. Jamie … well he was possibly worse. He made records at his home studio as The Jimmy C, playing all the instruments. Some of his music was used as the soundtrack for an American sexploitation cop show. Almost every week he would arrive with the new Jimmy C EP or LP, with finished artwork. He was an insanely good drummer too, and was able to combine that with vocals that were much, much stronger than mine. Murray played pretty basic but effective guitar, but perhaps more importantly, he had built a rehearsal studio in the warehouse where he ran his surveying business. The studio was five minutes' walk up the road from the house I was now sharing in North Fitzroy with an old friend, Jane. (Oh, yeah, I'd moved another two times.)

Inside the studio there was a bass amp, a speaker box, a bass guitar, and everything else I needed. Had there *not* been these benefits I would have had a quick think and given the idea a flat no. I may have been a glutton for punishment in some ways, strapping on a bass again, but at least I wasn't about to be hauling amplifiers up stairs anymore. At least I'd partially lost my passion and zeal. At least I was acting my age. All I needed now was a manila folder with lyrics in it. There was a lounge at the studio, there was beer, and usually chocolate if Jamie had some new kind of American 'candy' to test on us. And there was a convivial atmosphere. This by the way was the early 2010s.

(A few years on, Murray had to move, so he set up another studio, a better one, with recording facilities, indoor toilet, pool table and more.)

The setlist was … esoteric. It was all over the place, but that was the point really. It was a mixtape played live. Crowd-pleasers, and more obscure tunes that suited our abilities, tastes and humour. With two guitars and a drummer who could play the most upside down-sounding beats and time signatures, we were able to tackle tricky tunes like XTC's 'Making Plans For Nigel' and 'Jet' by Wings.

Targeted on our radar was the thirty-five to fifty-ish demographic, which meant that playing in the late afternoon on Sundays made sense. This suited us and suited the people who came along and wanted a drink and natter with friends with an eye to a late dinner and an early night before work on Monday. I was the only one with the time to promote the band, which was far less intensive work than it had been with other bands, but still needed doing, if only in the delivery of posters (which Jamie, a graphic artist would design for every show.) We played every three weeks or so, initially at The Marquis Of Lorne in Fitzroy which we all loved, but the place closed and, like most corner pubs, was refurbished and marketed again for young double-income couples who were colonising the renovated factories in the area.

We found a new home at the Town Hall Hotel in North Melbourne, a not dissimilar but slightly more rock'n'roll pub plastered with vintage posters and album covers. At most of our gigs we would see the same faces, which was good in the sense that our small but enthusiastic following always showed up, but not so satisfactory in the sense that there was a bit of a stasis, and the other guys didn't hassle their friends or friends of friends to bolster the numbers. (One of my fears with stand up was telling the same jokes to the same people – playing the same songs is not so problematic. Music as I mentioned has the ability to be familiar but no less enjoyable. We've all experienced the comfort of familiarity breeding contentment.)

Perhaps 2014 was the watershed year. It was the year that The TV Set split. The other guys were too busy. Murray was hiring the studio out so much we found it hard to practise in 'our' own rooms. The split was a kind of slow fade to black. We began playing less, practising less, and then it all just stopped altogether. I have to say I was a bit pissed off. I really enjoyed the gigs and the friendships. It was a bit like losing an arm.

I have a friend called Ash Naylor – although I haven't seen him in years and years. I met Ash when his band Even, played some gigs with Lust In Space in the mid-'90s. Both bands began playing in Melbourne at almost the same time. Ash was already a gifted guitarist in the Steve Marriot mode, and wrote catchy crunchy pop songs. Even went from strength to strength and are still one of the country's pre-eminent guitar rock bands. As Lust In Space disintegrated, Even strode on, releasing eight LPs and have yet to slow down. Ash meanwhile has been recruited to play guitar for the Countdown spectacular band, and spent a few years as a member of the Rockwiz 'orchestra'. He was recently asked to join the Church … which doesn't happen to a lot of us. He was in a band for a while with Michael from The TV Set, who is also a bit of a gun for hire. When the TV Set split, Michael's phone kept ringing. He can play guitar or drums. I feel like a nuff-nuff around him.

So let me measure my envy of Ash's talents and his career. Well, it's always been there, the jealousy, but early on I realised that the guy had a gift, and that whatever I could do, I couldn't do what he did, and virtually nobody else could. Virtuosity and versatility, as well as modesty. Ash looks the same now as he did in 1994. I think there's some sort of witchery going on. We would have made a good support band for Even, when they began to tour. Hanging off their coat-tails. Never really as good as them, but not dissimilar. (Even actually supported us at the launch of Speed Queen.) Maybe I coulda been a contender, but I never coulda been in the zone occupied by Ash.

30

It's gone now, all hope of programming Rage, that last chance to convert millennial fans of Spacey Jane and Boy and Bear and Lorde and the Kid Laroi to music featuring guitars, drums (rather than drums which trigger the bass, or drums sampled from 80s Casio toys), maybe keyboards being played by keyboard players, and authentically single-tracked vocals not fed through 50 shades of polarization and auto-tuning, and let's lose that machine which makes fart sounds too. How sad am I sounding right now? "Move aside grandpa and go back to the 1940s." Well, fair point, but then someone like Olivia Rodrigo comes along and I'm down a rabbit hole on YouTube watching her videos all night.

So listen up 'youth of today'; not only do you have new music in copious quantities and varying qualities to explore, you also have your parents' records, and perhaps even your grandparents' records. And with the current trend for vinyl, you probably have something to play them on. And you don't have to start with Elvis. You can start with Bach, or Frank Sinatra. But I'm not going to pick on you if you decide to go with Megan Thee Stallion instead.

We are in a strange space where Gorillaz (fronted by Damon Albarn, now in his thirtieth year of making music) are releasing records which are appealing to teenagers. And probably their parents, who wistfully tell their offspring about seeing Blur in 1994. The Gallagher Brothers seem to have found a new generation of fans, although Liam's longevity is a surprise. Perhaps the input of his rock star mates on that last LP has fortified his career. And that's what pop singers have these days. Careers. When Elvis was drafted in 1958 it was presumed his 'career' was over, and that his contemporaries would similarly turn into pillars of salt. You can make a career these days on the strength of one hit from another era. A Ha still play to massive crowds.

I've tried to be positive about what's happening now, given that pop is quite old with far fewer deviations to explore. I watch Rage. Yes, I do watch it, and I do hope I might find something appealing. That rarely happens. I do discover an artist now and then who 'isn't bad' but that's hardly enough to send me scurrying to the music shop to buy up. The only song that's blown me away in 2022 has been Jack White's 'What's the Trick'. It's been more than twenty years since White Stripes emerged. Jack White is now a 'heritage' artist. The Beatles (and hey, who else can win you any argument?) lasted eight years and by the time they were done, society had essentially gone from black and white and soaked in beer, to kaleidoscopic and dropping tabs of LSD. Pop music is not a vehicle of societal revolution anymore. It has little influence on philosophy or fashion. We are not likely to be shocked anymore. There's no lack of passion within fan bases, but who would the FBI keep a file on these days? Harry Styles?

Eight years ago, the world was precisely the same as it is now (for anyone over thirty.) Last year I heard Sleaford Mods for the first time – I like Sleaford Mods because they're genuinely scary, and it's not often you hope you never meet a *band* in a deserted alleyway – but in 2014 Sleaford Mods released their seventh album. Their *seventh*. I thought I was so *onto* Sleaford Mods – the sound of 2022 wasn't from 2022 at all.

I don't have anything *better* to do than follow the course of modern music, not better in a 'keeping busy' sense, but I do have other more *useful* things to do … like vacuuming, but I try to keep up, even when keeping up makes me wince in pain. This timeslip happens when I finally get round to watching films too; the brand new one from 2022 which is actually from … 2014 as well. I live in a time-warped world. It would be a cinch to differentiate a song and video from 1962 compared to a video and song from 1970. But songs from 2014 look and sound the same the same as songs from 2022. Genres have mutated a little but essentially it's a holding pattern. Acts tweak and experiment but they don't re-invent.

I've bought two CDs in the last ten years. A Sparks retrospective to fill at least some of the holes I've created by not keeping up with their prodigious output, and a Killers Best Of. To resort once more to the compilation CD is slightly ironic, but with my passion for music a little dimmed, I figured this release had all the hits I needed. The Killers are a slight anomaly, and yet contemporary enough to be one of the world's biggest bands, and I feel less ancient if I like them too. Every one of their seven studio LPs has gone to number 1 in the UK, and not far behind in the US and Australia. Their approach is poperatic incorporating elements of Brit-synth and large dollops of Springsteen's epic storytelling. The tunes are irresistible singalongs, and Brandon Flowers is a very likeable front guy. He's also a Mormon which is, frankly insane, and doesn't square with his band's completely secular approach. That is to say, Brandon's wacky beliefs don't infiltrate the music. But every time I watch him, I think, 'Really? Mormonism?' Ironically, his faith has prevented Brandon from becoming an asshole. No drug issues, no stumbling around drunk. Always on form. Almost too clean cut, but still less of a poseur than the guy from Panic! At The Disco who always looks like he's auditioning for Grease.

No band has soundtracked the sweet pain of teenage longing, loss and love, like The Killers. They do 'yearning' better than anyone except Bruce. On 'Just A Girl' Brandon sings, *"Why can't I sleep at night? / Why don't the moon look right / All of my friends say / She's just another girl / Don't let her stick it to your heart so hard."* There's barely a fifteen-year-old in the world who hasn't been in this place of exquisite emotional torture, with friends saying useless things. (And I do mean no band, because there *are* solo female artists who may not rock like The Killers, but whose break-up songs are crackers; Olivia Rodrigo is a specialist. You can only wonder where on earth her truisms and wisdom stems from since she's only in her early twenties, *'So when you gonna tell her that we did that, too? / She thinks it's special but it's all reused / That was the show we talked about / Played you the song she's singing / Do you get déjà vu when she's with you?'*

The Killers usually cover a song in concert originally recorded by an act from the country they're in, or sometimes just for the hell of it. Midnight Oil for example, and Icehouse and literally hundreds of others. The covers are largely love songs – Moon River is really pushing it though.

It's not just the existence of the Killers which heartens me in an arid time for what you might call traditional melodic stadium-friendly rock. It's also their popularity. People actually do have good taste now and then.

31

I returned to writing after The TV Set split and set about penning a book on the worst songs of The Beatles, persuasively named, *The Very Worst Of The Beatles*. It probably wasn't quite as easy as I thought it might be and the research was arduous. I didn't mind if Beatles fans didn't agree with me, but if I made factual errors that would have been fatal. It didn't sell that well, but I didn't have a major publisher's clout to help me along. I'm glad I did it. It wasn't exactly a chore to listen to a lot of Beatles songs. For the record, I think the worst of the worst was the band's cover of 'Everybody's Trying To Be My Baby', a Carl Perkins tune sung by Ringo and featuring an epic false start. A lot of the bad songs were drug-fuelled nonsense from later in the decade. But you have to dance nimbly around a soporific carnival of twaddle when it's possible heroin was to blame. Anyway, John Lennon wasn't about to pick up a copy of the book (and I'm pretty sure Paul McCartney hasn't either.)

Now that I spend so little time on procuring new music, I should really investigate the old music I missed – perhaps a deep dive into the Kinks' concept albums, or Fleetwood Mac before the band filled up with Americans, or the Creedence Clearwater Revival albums other than *Greatest Hits*, Steely Dan maybe or Isaac Hayes' *Hot Buttered Soul*. What about the strange and satirically-socialist world of Phil Ochs? Surely there are rewards hitherto undiscovered? And surely too these absolutely weren't the most compelling artists *you* were browsing for when you began your own musical journey. If you're fifteen and have the choice between Joni Mitchell and Thin Lizzy … well, do the Maths.

Seventy percent of record sales are now of 'heritage' acts. Queen have never been bigger. Fleetwood Mac, Elton John and

The Beatles of course are riding high. Elvis is at number thirty-two, and Creedence at fifty. Eminem's curtain call has been in the charts for five hundred and ninety-six weeks.

When a band like Primal Scream tours and relies heavily on a record released in 1990 (*Screamedelica*) no-one these days bats an eyelid. At least you could say they do have a new album … well it's four years old, but recent. The Stones were first deemed too old and too irrelevant in 1978, the year they released one of their best records ('Miss You'), then people began to view these never-ending bands, these reformations, these returns from dormancy as being perfectly acceptable. Ageism was out and nostalgia was in. Supergrass gave it a nine-year hiatus. (Their 'Best of", *Supergrass is 10*, came out in 2008.) Supergrass is now 24. No new album to promote, no real *reason* to play, except that people like to sing along to old Supergrass songs.

Almost every New Wave act exists in one form or another, often with only one original member, if that. The current iteration of The Jesus and Mary Chain at least boasts both the Reid brothers. You get the sense they're caught somewhere between revolution and showbiz. The gigs are nowhere near as chaotic as they were in the early days, but surliness is still a thing. Not really addressing the audience is still the band's schtick, and god forbid should anybody smile.

The only nonagenarian I can think of who still performed, until he died of what they call 'old age' was Pete Seeger. He was ninety-five. He looked pretty frail the last time I saw him. So, just how long can The Stones keep on with this? Charlie Watts was old, yes, but sitting down and keeping a simple (although perfect) rhythm pumping along is less ridiculous than Jagger doing his all to move the way he did in 1972. And yet he's pretty much got away with it so far. He's seventy-eight. He's thin, and he has hair. Both these things will dupe an audience into thinking he hasn't changed or aged, except on closer inspection his face looks like an alligator handbag. Can he pull this off at eighty-five? Keith Richards (seventy-eight) might say that some of the blues players kept at it well into their 80s. Yeah, but they were mostly sitting down.

Woodstock happened in 1969, and not one act at the festival had made records before 1965. At Glastonbury in 2022 Diana Ross appeared *sixty-one years* after the first Supremes single.

It's been thirty years since pop stars began to look a bit silly trying to fit into their tight pants at the outrageous age of … forty-eight maybe. Little did we know they'd never stop. Forty-eight, fifty-eight, sixty-eight …

Bearing all this in mind I did retire when The TV Set ended. Not because I felt too old. I just recognised that another band would be nowhere near as much fun as The TV Set, and that the band were essentially perfect. We were a gang and had our own secret way of talking, from Brian Wilson impersonations (me) to Simon Le Bon impersonations (Michael) to Paul Stanley impersonations (Jamie.) We spent most of our time falling about the place. I'd have to keep wrangling everyone back in to actually play some songs. It was a good way to go out. Having bags of fun in a rocking band the entire world would never hear of. Some of our gigs are on YouTube, but thankfully, they're virtually impossible to find.

32

You can't listen to music and read a book at the same time. You can't write and listen to an album. But you can drive and listen to music, and you can walk, run, and fall asleep to music. You can watch TV and listen to music if music is on the TV. The story of your life is most likely punctuated and organised and able to be in some small way revisited with the music that still stops you in your tracks.

I'm able to retrieve something of that feeling with music I like, but as far as music I've written, and bands I've been part of, the feeling is bittersweet. For me there isn't really a time in my own music career to return to in a nostalgic reverie. Not one that would meet my own standards of nailing it in that time and place in any case. I've experienced a bit of this and that certainly. Some nearlys, and indeed some deceptive moments of minor-pop-stardom. But if I'm ever forced to reveal the bands I've played in to anyone sufficiently quizzical, the best I have been able to get in return has been "Oh I've heard of that band" or "I might have seen you play once."

For every genuine fan from days gone by, there are ten gig-loiterers who may have seen us play once but can't quite say for certain (and millions of course for whom the bands were unknown, unseen and microscopic in their lack of fame.) This predicament, that of being a bit behind the peloton of comfortably successful acts, was never really resolved, not with the Fish, or Lust In Space, or the lesser groups I 'cut my chops' with. The unsung heroes. I gave it the best years of my lives and all I got was this lousy Fish John West Reject T shirt. I may have been thwarted in my own efforts at pop stardom but I guess I had a crack, and when I go, there will at least be some music, not all of it without merit, left behind as my legacy.

Last Christmas a friend bought me a magnificent LP-sized book about the Sex Pistols, featuring posters, news clippings, photos, recording schedules, and anything else you could imagine. If I was sixteen I would have been thrilled. If I was thirty I would have been thrilled. Now I'm considerably older and I was still thrilled. Only music (and books about music) can elicit this sort of feeling.

We cram our heads with so much music – how many tunes do you think you could at least hum along to? – that it's a wonder how there can be room in our brains, in our emotional cores, for anything else. Even if it wasn't God, be thankful that *someone* gave rock'n'roll to you.

About the Author

Michael Witheford was born in Sheffield, England and emigrated with his parents to Tasmania in 1965. Having relocated to Melbourne in the '80s he became a well-known music journalist and musician. Michael's first novel, *Buzzed* was published by Penguin in 2003. He is also the author of the *Very Worst Of The Beatles*, a comedic examination of the times the fab four got it wrong. Michael now lives in Launceston and is thinking about getting a new cat.

Michael's Rage Playlist ...

Cheap Trick – Southern Girls

The Records – Starry Eyes

The Raspberries – Go All The Way

Redd Kross – Jimmy's Fantasy

Aerosmith – Crazy

Blondie – X Offender

Sparks – This Town Ain't Big Enough

The Innocents – Sooner or Later

Urge Overkill – Sister Havana

Thin Lizzy – Chinatown

Divinyls – Siren

The Angels – Take A Long Line

Queen – Tie Your Mother Down

Deep Purple – Highway Star

Pop Will Eat Itself – Wise Up Sucker

The Fratellis – Chelsea Dagger

Elastica – Connection

Pulp – Do You Remember The First Time

The Wedding Present – Kennedy

Franz Ferdinand – Take Me Out

Falling Joys – Lock It

Manic Street Preachers – You Love Us

Beastie Boys – Hey Ladies

Eminem – Venom.

Wet Leg – UR Mum

HAIM – The Steps

MIA – Bad Girls

The Killers – Spaceman

Bee Gees – Nights On Broadway

Bee Gees – Don't Forget To Remember Me

Baccara – Yes Sir I Can Boogie

Nilsson – Without You

The Beach Boys – Don't Worry Baby

ABBA – The Winner Takes It All

Lynn Anderson – I Never Promised You A Rose Garden

The Reels – According To My Heart

Suede – Trash

ELO – Turn To Stone

Elton John – Goodbye Yellow Brick Road

Sex Pistols – Pretty Vacant

Hoodoo Gurus – Tojo

Violent Femmes – Add It Up

The Killjoys – Michael Told Me

Moondriven – Summer Comes

The Walker Brothers – The Sun Ain't Gonna Shine Anymore

Glen Campbell – Wichita Lineman

The Seekers – The Carnival Is Over